Careers in the Health Field

About four million people are employed in the rapidly-expanding medical-health field. Today the ratio of health workers to physicians is more than 200:1, and the health field offers over 300 different types of careers to suit a wide range of interests, talents and skills. Some require a baccalaureate degree or more, but the majority call for much shorter training periods in community colleges or on-the-job. This book offers an overview of the incredible variety of opportunities in this challenging and rewarding field—requirements, duties, salaries, potential for advancement and sources of further information.

Careers
‹ in the ›
Health Field

by
ESSIE E. LEE

Photographs

JULIAN MESSNER
NEW YORK

RILEY LIBRARY
OUACHITA BAPTIST UNIVERSITY

Published by Julian Messner
a division of Simon & Schuster, Inc.
1 West 39th Street, New York, N.Y. 10018
All Rights Reserved

Copyright © 1974, 1972 by Essie E. Lee

Revised Edition

Printed in the United States of America

Lee, Essie E
 Careers in the health field, by Essie E. Lee. New York, Messner [1972]

 191 p. illus. 22 cm. $4.95

 SUMMARY: Describes the variety of jobs available in the health field and discusses the necessary personal and academic qualifications.

 1. Medicine as a profession. 2. Public health as a profession.
[1. Medicine as a profession. 2. Public health as a profession.]
 I. Title.

R690.L38	610.69'5	74-9681
ISBN 0–671–32513–2 (lib. ed.)		MARC
Library of Congress	72 [4]	A C

FOREWORD

Health careers will provide an enormous potential for young people seeking to find a niche for themselves in the world of work in the 1970s and beyond.

The health "industry" is one of the most rapidly growing "industries" on the American scene.

Many factors underlie the rapid rise in demand for health care—population growth, increasing coverage under health insurance plans and the increasing scope of medical services. These factors are expected to continue to be a significant influence in expanding job opportunities for health service workers in the next few decades.

While population growth during the 1970s is expected to increase at a somewhat slower pace than during the past decade, there will be a disproportionate rise in those groups that generally require the most in the way of medical care—children under age five, elderly persons and urban dwellers in general. Technological developments are also expected to play an important role in contributing to the rise in demand for health workers. The broader scope of medical services now available through advances in medical science and technology are expected

CAREERS IN THE HEALTH FIELD

to provide continued expansion in the demand for new and existing types of health workers.

The total effect of these growth factors is expected to result in an increase in requirements for health workers from 3,900,000 in 1968 to about 6,400,000 in 1980. In addition, many new job opportunities will develop each year to replace those who retire, die or leave the field for other reasons.

Clearly, opportunities for work in the health field in the years ahead appear to be bright.

Almost everyone knows something about the professional services provided by doctors, dentists and pharmacists. Many also have some firsthand experience with the duties performed by nurses, attendants and other workers who take care of patients in hospitals. Less well known, however—but of great importance—is the work of large numbers of people employed behind the scenes in health service occupations.

Essie Lee, in this book, has performed a vital service in providing young people with a better understanding of the total spectrum of job opportunities that lie behind the more visible ones to which they may have been exposed some time during their lifetime. She probes behind the cold statistics, which alone are unlikely to have significant career influence on young people, to provide a striking description in simple, understandable terms of the functions involved in the delivery of medical services in today's world.

Foreword

This volume should be of enormous use to counselors and others working with young people in helping them to gain an understanding of the interest and excitement which can be found in the whole range of jobs in the health service sector. In particular, Dr. Lee should be commended for emphasizing the career development aspects of job opportunities in the health sector. Certainly, large numbers of people will be needed to fill the manpower requirements in the health sector during the decades ahead. Dr. Lee's exceedingly well-written and graphically descriptive book will be very useful in evoking the interest of young people toward helping to fill these requirements.

I can think of no other source which describes the range of occupations in the practical and functional way that Dr. Lee does and particularly so in terms of emphasis on the *teamwork* aspects of this family of jobs.

It is certainly to be hoped that this volume will receive wide distribution for the benefit of both the youngsters exposed and the manpower needs of this important growing sector of the American economy.

> Herbert Brenstock
> Regional Director
> U.S. Department of Labor

CONTENTS

FOREWORD   5

Introduction: WHO ARE THE "RELATED" OR SUPPORTIVE HEALTH PERSONNEL   15

One: THE LONGEST DAY   17

Two: EARN WHILE YOU LEARN   29

    Certified Laboratory Assistant
    Cytotechnologist
    Electroencephalograph (EEG) Technician
    Electrocardiograph (ECG) Technician
    Electromyograph (EMG) Technician
    Histologic Technician
    Medical Laboratory Technician
    Pathologist Assistant

Three: LIVE AND IN COLOR (A FIELD TRIP)   39

    Attendant
    Biochemical Equipment Technician
    Nurses' Aide
    Operating Room Technician

CAREERS IN THE HEALTH FIELD

    Orderlie
    Practical Nurse
    Registered Nurse
    Surgical Technician

Four: THE THERAPIES   48

    Occupational Therapy Assistant
    Orthopedic Assistant
    Orthotist
    Physical Therapy Technician
    Prosthetic Assistant
    Radiological Technologist—Radiotherapy
    Rehabilitation Therapist

Five: SOS ··· ——— ···   59

    Biomedical Equipment Assistant
    Cardiopulmonary Technician
    Inhalation Therapist
    Medical Emergency Technician
    Pharmacy Technician
    Radiological Technologist—X-Ray

Six: ROOM AND BOARD   72

    Administrative Dietitian
    Apprentice Cooks and Salad Men
    Area Supervisor—Housekeeping
    Assistant Manager—Laundry
    Assistant Supervisor—Laundry
    Broiler Cooks
    Diet Aide

Contents

Dietary Technician
Executive Chef
Executive Housekeeper
Extractors
Floor Waxer
General Cleaner
General Food Handler
Head Seamstress
Linen Room Handlers
Maids
Pantry Cook
Pullers
Packers
Salad Men
Sorters
Soup Cooks
Seamstress
Vegetable Cooks
Washers

Seven: KEEPING THE RECORD STRAIGHT   86

Computer Programmer
General Clerical Personnel
Medical Secretaries
Medical Transcribers
Steno/Typist
Typist/Clerk
Unit Clerk

Eight: THE FRONT DESK   99

Administrative Assistant in Charge of Patient Care
Admitting Clerk

CAREERS IN THE HEALTH FIELD

    Addressograph Plate Man
    Chief Reservation Clerk
    Doorman
    Elevator Operator
    I.V., or Intravenous, Nurse
    Medical Assistant
    Messenger
    Preadmitting Clerk
    Public Health Nurse
→ Social Worker
    Transporter

Nine: SAFE AND SOUND

    Air-Conditioning Installer and Maintenance
    Chief Purchasing Agent
    Chief of Maintenance and Engineering
    Chief Security Officer
    Central Supply Assistant
    Carpenters
    Electricians' Helper
    Floor Buffer
    Furniture Mover
    Furniture Repair and Refinisher
    Locksmith
    Light Man
    Maintenance Men
    Metal Cleaner and Polisher
    Office Machine Serviceman
    Painter—Foreman
    Painter
    Plasterer
    Refrigeration Mechanic

Contents

    Security Guard
    Shade and Drapery Man
    Supervisor—Central Supply
    Television Service and Repairman
    Tile Worker and Tile Setter
    Touch-Up Painter
    Utilities Mechanic

Ten: COMMUNICATIONS   129

    ➟Assistant—Public Relations Officer
    Chief Hospital Administrator
    Chief Medical Record Librarian
    Executive Secretary
    Hyperbaric Chamber Operator
    Medical Record Librarian
    Medical Record Technician
    Page Operator
    Projectionist
    Photographer
    ➟Public Relations Officer
    Printing Assistant
    Receptionist
    Switchboard Operator
    Volunteers

Eleven: AUXILIARY SERVICES   144

    Account Representative
    Biller
    Cashier
    Child-Care Technician
    Control Clerk
    City Investigator

CAREERS IN THE HEALTH FIELD

    Community Health Aide
    Coordinator of Employee Health Service
    Director—Patients' Accounts
    Pediatric Assistant
    Psychiatric Aide
    Psychiatric Technician
    Secretary/Typist
    Social Work Technician
    Therapeutic Recreational Assistant

Twelve: OUT IN THE COMMUNITY   158

    Administrator—Nursing Home
    Coordinator—Nursing Home
    Director of Nurses—Nursing Home
    Employment Counselor
    Family Health Worker
    Family-Planning Counselor
    Food Products Inspector
    Food Service Inspector
    Home Health Aide
    Health Engineering Assistant
    Health Laboratory Technician
    Orthoptist
    Optician
    Optician Technician
    Sanitary Inspector
    Teacher Aide

LOOKING AHEAD   174

SOURCES OF FURTHER INFORMATION   178

INDEX   189

INTRODUCTION
Who Are the "Related" or Supportive Health Personnel?

Out of every 100 health workers, only nine are physicians. Another 18 are in medically related occupations; seven are in the dental profession and services; 50 are in nursing categories; six in environmental health sciences; and 10 in all other health occupations. In 1900, the ratio of all health workers to physicians was 60:1. Today that ratio is more than 200:1. Heart surgery may require the services of as many as 18 or 20 differently specialized people. Like the seven-eighths of the iceberg that never shows above the waterline, many essential people with special skills requiring precise training work daily behind the scenes unknown to the patient.

The health field offers a variety of careers to suit individual interests, talents and skills. More than 300 separate identifiable kinds of work are found among medical and health professions and occupations. Although some require a baccalaureate degree or more, the majority call for a much shorter training period. For example, the

CAREERS IN THE HEALTH FIELD

community colleges offer associate degree programs in more than 40 health-related fields. Many other jobs need only high-school graduation and on-the-job training. Most of the new occupations are in the "aide," "assistant," and "technician" level—the allied health field.

By joining the health team, you will be working toward a common goal of optimum health care for all people. You will find that the allied professional's job not only provides a challenging and rewarding experience but offers security, stimulating work, opportunity for advancement and deep personal satisfaction.

Ninety-four years ago Benjamin Disraeli, the first Earl of Beaconsfield, said: "The health of the people is really the foundation upon which all their happiness and all their powers as a state depend." This statement is as accurate in 1972 as it was in 1877. Our story of Stephen Bowman's hospitalization helps you identify the important role of supportive medical personnel, the paraprofessionals.

One ▶

THE LONGEST DAY

The pain was unbearable! How long had it been since someone called for that ambulance? Steve lay on his back, eyes shaded by his sweating hand, and groaned softly. What bad luck! Just two weeks before the Regional Tournament and now a broken leg! For a moment, his thoughts raced ahead to the starting game and anticipation blotted out throbbing pain. He dozed briefly, but the screaming siren startled him awake. A policeman was assisting a uniformed man with a stretcher. Steve was able to read the words *Medical Emergency Technician* in red letters against the white uniform. Gently but swiftly they secured the splint, and Steve was rolled into the ambulance.

During the ride to the hospital, sounds of adult conversation drifted above him. It was Jim, the technician, talking with Coach Reynolds. "Looks like a bad compound fracture. . . . That's why I'm using these sterile pads. Lowering the head will help prevent shock.

That's right. . . . Let's keep him loosely covered!"

Steve stirred once as the ambulance sped along the tree-lined boulevard toward Tri-City Hospital. The sound of screeching tires turning into the driveway roused him. The ambulance stopped abruptly, and its doors flew open. Two blue-uniformed *Attendants* ran forward and took charge of the stretcher. Within minutes, Steve was lifted and wheeled into a brightly lit room which seemed like a kaleidoscope of bodies and equipment. Coach Reynolds gave him a reassuring nod as Jim reported briefly to a young man wearing a white jacket with a nameplate. Steve couldn't make out the name, but beneath it in large letters were the words *Senior Resident*. The young man's face seemed friendly but concerned. Glancing toward Steve, he said, "Your parents are on the way, but meanwhile we'll give you something to ease the pain."

He gave an order, and a pretty nurse approached the table. She winked at Steve and said, "You'll hardly feel it—don't worry." She was right. He felt a slight pressure and a pin prick on his right upper arm.

Steve was beginning to doze again when he recognized his father's familiar voice. Dr. Mike Perkins, the senior resident, was explaining the treatment procedure to his father. There would be x-rays, blood and other tests and, finally, surgery. Even at this moment, his family physician was in touch with a specialist. As they talked about his future, Steve sensed detachment; he was like an on-

The Longest Day

looker, an observer, one of those many uniforms viewing "the leg." There seemed to be so many people—nurses, doctors, aides, orderlies, technicians, messengers and others he couldn't recognize. Each had a job, but each seemed to be part of some unified effort. He compared them with his own pals on the basketball team: he wondered if they had practice sessions too! Steve's mother bent down and kissed his tear-streaked cheek. His father patted him on the shoulder. Steve wanted to ask them some questions, but his lips couldn't form the words. He was surrendering to the medication, drifting off into deep sleep.

"Hi, Steve! Wake up! Come on, Steve!" He could hear, but he had difficulty responding to the voices. He saw them indistinctly peering down at him and felt their hands shaking his shoulders.

"It must be evening," he thought. "The shades are drawn. How many hours ago did Stephen Bowman, a 16-year-old junior at Aldrich High School, star forward of the varsity basketball team, fracture his right thigh bone?"

"I'm Janice Bard, a *Student Nurse*." Steve squinted at a young round face, not much older than his. He still couldn't see her clearly, but the voice was pleasant. Steve heard that Miss Bard and intern Dave Mann were ready to formally admit him to Faulkner Wing 8 with a complete physical examination.

When the curtains were drawn back after the comple-

CAREERS IN THE HEALTH FIELD

tion of the examination, Steve was able to look around the room. He saw immediately that he had a roommate—a very sick roommate! There were bottles hanging overhead, tubes protruding from under the sheets and a huge plastic canopy covering the head of the bed. Dr. Mann saw the look of panic on Steve's face. "It looks worse than it is; don't be alarmed," he said quietly. "He'll be up and about in a day or two." Steve was not at all convinced, but he was too tired to say so, and he had little time to be concerned about it. There was a sudden flurry of movement at the door. He turned toward that sound. A stout man dressed in green was hurrying to Steve's bedside. His nameplate read "Tom Brennan, *Prep Team*." "Hello there! Are you Stephen Bowman? I'm Brennan from the operating room. My job is to get you ready for the surgical team." Brennan talked, and Steve cautiously watched him assemble razor, soap, cotton balls and towels. "I'm going to shave and wash your leg and lower trunk so that they will be as clean as possible. This helps to prevent infection." As the razor made sweeping paths through the mounds of lather down his leg, Steve was reminded of the skiing trip that he would miss. He was so disappointed! Two months of planning and practice wasted! Brennan was thorough and went about his work with quick, sure strokes. "There you go now, all nicely cleaned up," he said as he wrapped fresh linen towels about Steve's injured leg.

"Do you have the specimen ready?" Steve did and

The Longest Day

handed over the bright blue urinal to the *Orderlie*. "See you around," called Brennan from the door.

As he left, a very feminine, laughing voice was heard. "Are you following me? Brennan, you're everywhere!" Steve looked expectantly toward the door and saw a mass of long black hair and friendly black eyes. "I'm Sue Wong, *Laboratory Technician*. I have to take a little blood for some important preoperative tests." She swabbed Steve's left forearm, inserted the needle and drew her samples. She filled four small tubes and pressed an alcohol sponge to the puncture site as she withdrew the needle.

Dr. Mann peeked in. "We're about ready, Steve. You'll make a stop at x-ray, and then on to surgery." His parents moved quickly into the room. His mother's eyes were red and swollen, but she was smiling. His father's voice seemed strained. "Don't worry, son; they're going to take good care of you. Dr. Jenkins is up there now conferring with the surgeon. We'll be right here waiting for you!" His mother tried to reach over and touch him, but the stretcher was pushed between them.

"OK, Dad, I'm all right—really I am." Steve hoped that his voice didn't shake too much. He wouldn't want his parents to know how scary this whole thing was. The *Operating Room Attendant* half lifted him onto the stretcher, and Miss Bard ticked off items from her check list as she escorted them to the elevator.

"Here's the chart—everything checks!" She lightly

patted Steve's blanketed head and looked straight into his eyes. "We're having cake and ice cream later. I'll save yours, so don't be too long!" She put her fingers to her lips and pressed them to Steve's forehead. The starched wings at the back of Miss Bard's cap were the last thing Steve saw before the heavy iron doors of the elevator clanged shut.

Mrs. Florence Byers, *Nurse in Charge,* flopped down wearily on the stool facing her corner desk. The recovery room looked like a disaster area! Practically every piece of emergency equipment had been needed today! Two *Operating Room Technicians* were busy cleaning, assembling and storing the many lifesaving devices. Four of the 12 beds were still occupied, but two patients appeared ready to return to their rooms. Although she had been on duty for 12 hours, Mrs. Byers would stay until the young man with the fracture was fully awake. "How are his vital signs [blood pressure, pulse and respiration rates]?" Mrs. Byers asked of the green-garbed figure holding Steve's wrist. "They're within normal range—he'll be awake soon," a basso-deep voice replied. The voice belonged to Keith Downey, *Practical Nurse.* Keith was proud to be a member of the recovery room staff. From his three-year stint as an Army Medical Corps man in Vietnam, Keith had gained valuable experience and the incentive to earn a practical nurse diploma. He carefully went through the routine of inspecting Steve's cast, regulating the flow of intravenous fluid and examining protruding toes.

A smile slowly spread across Mrs. Byers's face, momentarily relaxing the lines of tension. She watched Keith's thorough and gentle performance and thought to herself, "Someday he'll achieve his goal. What a fine doctor he'll make!"

Steve stirred and attempted to turn onto his left side. He couldn't quite make it, because something heavy seemed to be holding him down. Steve opened his eyes and slowly looked around the large room. "This must be the recovery room that Bob, the *X-ray Technician,* had talked about," he thought. Bob had tried to relieve Steve's apprehension with explanations of the process used in the speedy development of his eight pictures. Steve, an amateur photographer, learned a couple of things to try out later, and Bob promised to help him with a couple of pictures for a national film contest.

After his short ride along a quiet corridor to the operating room, Steve recognized the bulky form of Dr. Jenkins standing at the entrance. "Trying to get an extra vacation—eh, Steve? It won't work. This hospital has teachers," he teased. Steve was introduced to the surgeon, Dr. Cushney, and the two doctors briefly described the planned surgical procedure to him. Steve followed their discussion with interest, although he couldn't understand much of it. However, Dr. Jenkins had known Steve all of his 16 years, and it felt good knowing that the doc-

CAREERS IN THE HEALTH FIELD

tor would be with him. The stretcher pushed through a door marked Anesthesia.

Three *Surgical Technicians* stood before a low sink briskly scrubbing their arms and hands; one appeared to be a girl. Their strange green coveralls seemed to end in large boots, but their eyes were laughing above the surgical masks. "We will assist your doctor during the operation," explained the girl. "Are you a nurse?" Steve asked. "No; she's not," replied one of the young men. "We used to be *Nurses' Aides* before we enrolled in the hospital's 18-month course for Surgical Technicians." Steve watched them in fascination. The rivulets of clear water running down their arms made crooked paths through thick soapsuds. With arms extended forward, the technicians stepped into long green gowns held by three *Attendants*. Steve remembered that Dr. Amos, the anesthetist, had entered the room as the green-garbed figures silently glided out. The doctor seemed very tall to Steve, over six feet. Steve wondered if he too had been an athlete.

Dr. Amos seemed to read Steve's thoughts. "No. I was never a basketball player. I used to ski, though, and I broke a couple of legs in my time."

Steve was becoming sleepy again, but he heard Dr. Amos' reply to his question "When will I go to sleep?"

"Before you can count to 10," Dr. Amos had said.

He had reached three, and now he was waking up. Steve's moving about hadn't gone unnoticed. Mrs. Byers

The Longest Day

removed her starched, pleated cap, pulled a heavy, navy cardigan about her shoulders and called out to Keith—"See you in the morning"—before she carefully closed the door behind her.

Miss Bard remembered to save ice cream and cake for Steve, but he asked for a rain check. All he wanted now was sleep. His parents watched anxiously as he was carefully shifted from stretcher to bed by the operating room attendant and the orderly. Before Miss Bard adjusted the covers, the *Orthopedic Assistant* placed small sandbags along the sides of the long white cast to keep the leg in an upright position.

Pointing to a steel apparatus above Steve's bed, Glen, the assistant, said, "That trapeze will help you move about in bed more freely. Just grab the bar with one or both hands and lift your body. I'll come back tomorrow and we'll practice." Steve nodded drowsily. His parents were waiting to say goodnight. They seemed more relaxed now. Drs. Jenkins and Cushney had assured them of a complete recovery.

Sandy Miles, the *Nurses' Aide,* removed the thermometer from Steve's mouth, read it and shook it vigorously before replacing it in its bedside container. She fluffed up the pillows, wiped Steve's face with a cool damp cloth and raised the bed's side-rails. "This button is your call light. Just press it, and someone will answer through the intercom," she explained. "It's after eight o'clock, so you'll probably sleep through the night. Good night, for

CAREERS IN THE HEALTH FIELD

now." Miss Miles busied herself with the other patient for a few moments before she raised the window, dimmed the light and closed the door.

"It's been a long day, and now it's so quiet after all the excitement," Steve thought. The room's furnishings cast weird-looking shadows on the walls and ceiling. Steve studied them for a few minutes. Then he yawned, and almost immediately fell asleep.

It was afternoon visiting hours on Faulkner Wing 8, and Steve's parents were seated next to his bed. They were listening intently to Steve's report of the morning's activities. "First the orderlie woke me up early; he took my temperature and helped me wash up. Then it was time for breakfast, and the *Diet Aide* opened the eggs for me. But I managed alone at lunch." Steve paused and gestured toward the other bed. The *Inhalation Therapist* had removed the oxygen tent, so Steve could see and talk with the other patient now. "Mom! Dad! I want you to meet Andy Rosado. He's got diabetes!" Steve revealed.

Andy, a sophomore at State University, had been a diabetic for two years. However, he had made the mistake of trying to make all the parties and social events of the university's Winter Carnival and had become acutely ill. Fortunately, he had responded well to treatment and would be discharged in a week or two. "Pleased to meet you," the dark-haired youth said, extending his hand to Mr. Bowman. "Steve's right—it has been hectic around here. Miss Wong took blood from both of us for tests. The *Orthopedic Assistant* taught Steve how to use the trapeze. He brought along the *Physical Therapy Assistant,* who took measurements for Steve's crutches. The *Social Work Technician* came in just before lunch. She's sending the medical reports to the Health Services offices at each of our schools. Miss Arrington, the *Dietary Technician,* left food charts from which I must practice selecting and planning menus for a week." Andy dramatically threw his arms up in the air, demonstrating total exasperation, and fell back on the pillows feigning exhaustion. The Bowmans joined him in laughter. They could relax now, confident that Andy's sense of humor would lessen the shock of Steve's first hospitalization.

During the following week, Steve had the opportunity to meet other members of the supportive health team. For example, on one of his visits to the Department of Rehabilitation Services, he watched an *Occupational Therapy Aide* demonstrate specially designed kitchen utensils to a group of handicapped women. Another time, a young girl was being fitted for a back brace by the *Orthotic Technician.* Dr. Cushney, the orthopedic surgeon, and the technician were collaborating on the adjustments to be made, and graciously explained some of the techniques employed in the manufacture of corrective devices.

One of the people who impressed Steve most was Fred Fulton, the *Ward Manager.* Mr. Fulton served as the

CAREERS IN THE HEALTH FIELD

administrator for Faulkner Wings 8 and 9. He had enlisted in the U.S. Navy when he was a high-school junior. For more than three years, his assignment was as ship's clerk. Meanwhile, he earned his high-school diploma. After his discharge, Mr. Fulton attended evening classes at the local community college. His courses in business administration and the behavioral sciences, coupled with his navy experience, qualified him for the hospital's on-the-job training program. Mr. Fulton enjoyed his job of teaching and training clerical personnel, supervising patient services and maintaining all nonmedical functions.

A week later, Mr. and Mrs. Bowman came to take Steve home. The *Social Service Aide* arranged for the ambulance to transport him, a hospital bed for home use, visiting nurse services and follow-up clinic visits. Steve and Andy, amid noisy good-byes, promised to write to each other and many of their new friends at Tri-City Hospital. As the ambulance pulled out of the driveway, Steve looked back toward the hospital and remembered some of the happy and sad experiences of the past two weeks. "It's wonderful to be going home," he said to no one in particular.

Two ▶

EARN WHILE YOU LEARN

In our first chapter, we met a few of the supportive personnel who assisted in the treatment and care of Steve Bowman. There are many, many more.

Suppose we take a look at some of the careers in "The Quiet Zone," the modern hospital. It is Monday morning in the personnel office of Tri-City Hospital. David Welpin, *Personnel Director,* is looking over the day's schedule. It is a typical Monday schedule, very full!

"Are you ready for your first appointment?" his secretary inquires. "He's a high-school graduate whose courses included two years of mathematics and a year each of biology and chemistry," she reports.

"Any previous hospital experience?" Mr. Welpin asks.

"No, but according to his references he's a conscientious, reliable worker. I'll send him in now."

Gilbert Carter shook hands with Mr. Welpin and sat down in the chair beside the desk. Gilbert liked working with people, and wanted some job security and a career with a promise of advancement. Mr. Welpin continued to read Gilbert's application for a few minutes. "You're still quite young. Perhaps you would like to hear about our training programs," offered Mr. Welpin, pointing to a large wall chart picturing the hospital's organizational framework. Aware of Gilbert's interests, skills and possible potential, Mr. Welpin chose the training program in one area of the hospital's clinical occupations, bioelectrical monitoring—the process of observing and/or recording the electrical potential produced by various systems of the body with the use of highly specialized technical equipment.

"One such piece of equipment," Mr. Welpin said, "is the ECG or EKG machine, which records heart actions. The operator of this machine is called an *Electrocardiograph Technician*. He may work in clinical settings or at the patient's bedside, depending upon whether or not the patient's condition permits transportation to the department." Gilbert nodded, indicating that he understood.

"Have you ever heard of an EEG, or electroencephalograph test?" Mr. Welpin asked, pointing to another section of the wall chart. Without waiting for an answer, he continued: "The *EEG Technician* is trained to operate an instrument which records brain waves. He also receives training which enables him to recognize the acute symptoms of patients, such as convulsive seizures,

Earn While You Learn

which may occur during the test and need prompt medical assistance." Gilbert moved closer and read that this technician's training period was usually longer than most others. He also noticed that instruction in biomedical electronics might be necessary to qualify for higher positions.

"Science and mathematics were my favorite subjects in high school—this EEG technician interests me," he told Mr. Welpin.

"An EEG technician must be interested in the patient's well-being. Patients who need an EEG vary from the very ill hospital patient to the ambulatory one who comes to the clinic for examination. A technician must be able to make all patients feel at ease and offer reassurance when they are worried or tense. If the technician is good, a patient will feel so relaxed that he may fall asleep during the examination."

"Do you need a license?" Gilbert asked.

"After the technician completes the training course, he must complete a year of EEG instruction and laboratory experience. He or she can then apply for certification to the American Board of Registration of Electroencephalographic Technologists (ABRET). The technician must provide evidence to the board that he has personally recorded 1,000 EEGs, and then successfully pass a two-part EEG examination. He is then qualified to call himself a registered EEG technologist and use the initials R.E.T. after his name.

CAREERS IN THE HEALTH FIELD

"There's one more possibility in this group; it is called electromyography. An *EMG Technician* assists the doctor in recording and analyzing bioelectrical impulses which originate in muscle tissues. He assists the doctor with patient care, prepares, catalogues and files reports. At times, he may help with other neurological tests or research programs."

Gilbert continued to read from the chart and saw that all three positions required high-school graduation. Hospital on-the-job training conducted by doctors or senior technicians continued as long as one year, depending upon the trainee's background and experience. Gilbert, 23 years old, planned to marry within a year; he needed a position which would support a family. "What are the beginning salaries?"

Mr. Welpin flipped open a large reference book on the desk. "They averaged $6,100 to $7,500 in early 1974. More than half of all technicians working for the Federal Government in 1973 earned over $8,500, and a few earned as much as $10,500 a year. Salaries in large institutions tend to be higher." Turning away from the book, he said, "Tri-City begins at $8,500, with periodic raises. Technicians generally work a 35-to-40-hour week, which may include work on weekends, and there are opportunities for part-time employment. Technicians working in hospitals receive the same fringe benefits as other hospital personnel. Tri-City assists with tuition costs or provides free courses for employees interested in moving up the career ladder."

The ringing of the telephone interrupted their conversation. It was Mr. Welpin's secretary, telling him of an emergency situation in another part of the hospital. "You'll have to excuse me for a few minutes. I hope it won't take long. While I'm away, why don't you get acquainted with my next applicant? His career search is similar to yours." He dialed his secretary. "Please send in Mr. Donald Perkins."

Donald Perkins had acquired 30 college credits during his freshman year at State University. His mother's illness and subsequent death had forced him to leave school and seek work; the Perkinses were a tightly knit group and Donald, the eldest son, felt obligated to help his father provide for the six younger Perkinses.

"I'm Dave Welpin, Personnel Director," Mr. Welpin introduced himself. "I'd like for you to meet Gilbert Carter. He too is looking for a career in the health sciences."

Gilbert rose and offered his right hand to Donald. "Pleased to meet you," he said hesitantly but with a wide grin.

"You fellows may look over this material on careers in medical laboratory while I'm away," said Mr. Welpin, handing Gilbert a package of pamphlets, sheets, catalogues and pictures.

"What kind of work are you looking for?" asked Gilbert.

CAREERS IN THE HEALTH FIELD

Donald was leafing through the material left by Mr. Welpin. "I don't really know, but this laboratory work might be a beginning," he replied. "Listen to this: '*Certified Laboratory Assistant* collects blood specimens from patients, prepares and stains slides for microscopic organisms, groups and types blood, examines urine and body fluids under the microscope and concentrates specimens for parasitologic study. This technician is trained to use precision instruments, like electronic counters. Assistants may also perform blood tests to determine bleeding or coagulation time. Many more assistants are needed to perform the many tests that modern doctors rely upon. Although women dominate this field, this is a good entry-level position for men. Laboratory assistants receive one year of practical and technical training which includes at least 100 hours of classroom instruction in addition to 40 to 44 hours a week of laboratory training.' "

Gilbert nodded his head vigorously. "Not bad. . . um . . . not bad, and Tri-City operates a school approved by the A.M.A. [American Medical Association]."

" 'The *Histologic Technician* requires only a high-school background and then a year's training in a pathology laboratory,' " Donald continued.

"What does he do?" Gilbert inquired.

"It says here that he cuts frozen sections of body tissue very thin, mounts them on slides and stains them with special dyes."

Gilbert appeared startled and wide-eyed. "If it's in the morgue, count me out!" he declared.

Donald chuckled and said, "No—it looks like he works in a pathology laboratory."

"That's much better." Gilbert sighed with relief and assumed a more relaxed position in the chair.

" 'The position of histologic technician may be a career in itself,' " Donald continued, " 'or it can serve as training for more advanced positions in the field of medical technology.' "

"I plan to resume my education at night. I could work toward an associate degree in the field of *Medical Laboratory Technician.* The medical laboratory technician performs tests in urinalysis, hematology, serology, bacteriology and clinical chemistry. After graduation, I'll be eligible to take the registry examination of the American Medical Technologists. If I pass it, I can sign my name Donald Perkins, M.L.T."

Gilbert was impressed. "Perhaps I could take some evening courses, too. I'm getting married soon, but my girl will work until I'm settled."

Donald handed him several sheets from the package. "Look these over. They require two years of college plus one year of specialized training. All of these laboratory positions call for one to have a quick mind, deft hands for working with delicate glassware and fragile instruments and a sense of efficiency."

" 'The *Cytotechnologist,*' " Gilbert read, " 'is capable

of recognizing minute abnormalities in color, size and shape of cell substances. He uses special dyes to stain a sample of cell cytoplasm and nucleus for study under the microscope.'" He paused momentarily, and his thoughts drifted back to his high-school Biology 2 class; he recalled the thrill of discovering and identifying the smears under the lens. Mr. Michaels, his teacher, was always amazed at Gilbert's professional handling of the microscope.

"You use that equipment like a true scientist," he once said to Gilbert.

Gilbert left his daydreaming and continued reading from the sheets. " 'Cytotechnologists are needed to screen cervical smears for early detection of cancer. Moreover, the use of cytology is increasing in detecting cancer of the lung, stomach and other body sites. This technician may work in private laboratories and in research facilities, as well as in hospitals. As early detection methods for cancer through cytologic smears are increasingly used, the need for this specialist continues to grow at the rate of 1,000 annually. Licensure is not required. However, the Registry of Medical Technologists of the American Society of Clinical Pathologists gives the professional certification of CT (ASCP) to graduates of American Medical Association–approved programs who pass the certifying examination. Anyone considering this career should have a quiet, patient temperament, concern for details and precision, good eyesight and a willingness to work sometimes alone, sitting at the micro-

Earn While You Learn

scope for many hours.'"

"Here Donald," Gilbert said suddenly. "I like them warm and breathing!" Gilbert thrust the sheets toward Donald.

Donald saw the heading *Pathologists' Assistant* and doubled up with laughter. "It only means that after two years of college and one year of hospital training, you are ready to assist in postmortem examinations. Your reward is a nice 'quiet place' to work!" Sounds of hearty laughter reached Mr. Welpin from the outer office. He had been gone longer than expected, so he was pleased that the two had discovered some mutual interest.

"I think my eventual goal will be a medical technologist in a blood bank," Donald said to Mr. Welpin. "Meanwhile, I'd like to begin by enrolling in the hospital's laboratory assistant course." Mr. Welpin nodded and continued making notes.

"You'll be paid $50 a week as a trainee," he said to Donald. "What about you, Gilbert? Can we help you?"

"Yes . . . I guess," Gilbert said thoughtfully. "The lab work interests me too, but I would like a little more time to think about it, and talk it over with my fiancée."

"You're perfectly right. Choosing a career is a serious matter." Mr. Welpin rose and came from behind his desk. "We're showing a film of the hospital this morning to new employees. It's called *'The Quiet Zone.'* It shows how our large, complex institution functions so smoothly

CAREERS IN THE HEALTH FIELD

because of the help and cooperation of more than 50 different categories of employees. Why don't you stop by the auditorium and see it? It might help Gilbert with his decision."

Mr. Welpin led them to the outside door. He returned to his office and glanced at his watch. Most of the day was still ahead! It was only 10:00 A.M.

Three ▶

LIVE AND IN COLOR
(A Field Trip)

"Why did you decide to become a nurse, Miss Bard?" a round-faced, serious-looking girl wanted to know. Miss Bard was participating in "Open House Week," held annually by the hospital for high-school students.

"I had wanted to study medicine, but then the training was too long. During my senior year at Saint Catherine's High School, I volunteered for a school project in a home for the aged. I was assigned to work with elderly blind people. That was a very happy year for me; I received so much personal satisfaction helping others that I decided to make it a career."

The group of students leaned forward drawn by the excitement in her voice. "What's the difference between a *Registered Nurse* and a *Practical Nurse?*" a short, stout girl wearing thick-lensed glasses asked.

"Professional or registered nurses are vital members of the medical team. Acting under the direction of a physician, registered nurses or R.N.s plan the patients'

CAREERS IN THE HEALTH FIELD

nursing care not only in the hospital but also in the physician's office. Nursing combines the aspects of service and science; the field offers a variety of career opportunities. In a hospital setting, the R.N. may work with a diversified group of patients ranging from newborn infants to seriously ill cardiac or heart patients. Duties of hospital nurses may fall between direct patient care, supervision of other nursing personnel and education." Miss Bard suddenly interrupted her breathless narration with a nervous giggle. Caught up in her own enthusiasm, she realized that she had forgotten to answer the student's question.

"The training period is longer and the responsibilities greater for the R.N. For example—the training program includes experience in all aspects of medicine, such as psychiatry, community health, contagious diseases, obstetrics and pediatrics. Relevant course work accompanies this experience, and a student learns about nutrition, pharmacology, maternal and child nursing and public health. Education for practical nurses generally consists of one year of study following high-school graduation. Practical nurses usually work under the supervision of a registered nurse."

A tall, thin girl with long toffee-colored hair raised her hand. "Where else can nurses work besides hospitals?"

"If you look at your pamphlet, you'll see that institutions, camps, industry, schools, clinics, nursing homes and public health agencies are all possibilities."

Live and in Color

A heavy-set teen-age boy standing near the back of the group asked, "Does Tri-City Hospital train registered nurses?"

"Yes; this hospital has a school for nurses and offers a three-year course, but training for varying periods is available at community colleges and universities. Men are finding nursing to be an exciting career, because of the opportunities for professional advancement and specialization. After receiving your education, to use the initials R.N. (registered nurse) or L.P.N. (licensed practical nurse) and practice the profession, the graduate of an approved school of nursing must pass an examination for licensure in most states."

"Could you tell us about the salaries?" an athletic-looking Black boy asked.

"Yes. Most recent graduates without experience begin with an annual salary of about $10,000. Licensed practical nurses would earn less, about $8,500."

"Are the hours long?" the same young man wanted to know.

"We have an eight-hour shift and work five days a week. Nurses care for patients round the clock, so we have day, afternoon and night shifts. Some hospitals offer higher pay for the afternoon and nights shifts, because they're less attractive," Miss Bard reported. "But remember, to be a good nurse and enjoy your work, you must like all people, be adaptable and alert, have an excellent memory and be able to respond intelligently in an emergency!" Miss Bard started to sit down but hesitated a moment to add: "Oh. I forgot! You need strong feet!" The students joined her in laughter.

Mr. Kurt Simon, the students' guidance counselor, rose and faced the group. "You noticed that Miss Bard spoke of 'careers,' not 'jobs.' 'Job' reminds you of work; day in, day out, the same routine, get the check on Friday, punch in on Monday, etc., etc. 'Career' brings to mind excitement, challenge, professionalism, using your skills and your mind, direct contact with the people you are helping." Gesturing toward a colorfully dressed group at the nurses' station, he suggested: "Let's meet some of the people who assist the nurses."

One of them, carrying a tray, moved out from the group and approached Miss Bard. She was Miss Sandy Miles, *Nurses' Aide*. "You may have sodas or coffee with your sandwiches and cookies," she announced, walking among the students.

"Where did you get your training?" a small girl with a long ponytail sitting up front asked Miss Miles.

"I graduated from a technical high school, where I was a health careers major; all the basic skills for my position were learned there. After a year, I plan to begin training for a practical nurse. The hospital encourages up-grading, so I will continue to receive full pay, although I will be in class half of the time." Sandy smiled at the girl and returned to passing the tray.

"Have you met Henry, our *Orderlie?* He's a key member of our team." Miss Bard beckoned toward two young men near the utility room. Henry wore a bright-blue uniform which contrasted sharply with George's dark-gray *Attendant's* jacket. With quick, long strides, they reached Miss Bard's side. Henry, the shorter, acted as spokesman.

"George and I were trained here on the job; we graduated from high school by taking courses at night, because we were dropouts. We assist in the care of patients by performing such tasks as dressing, feeding and bathing, bed making, stretcher delivery and routines essential to the comfort of patients. Nurses teach and supervise us."

"Do you only take care of male patients?"

"No, we help with all the patients; we are really helpful in lifting disabled or heavy patients from the bed or chair."

George turned and nudged Henry. "Don't forget to tell them that we work all over the hospital, every service. The best place is pediatrics, I think, because I like children." Everyone was amused, because George's more than six feet and 200 pounds–plus made him look somewhat like a giant wrestler. A grin suddenly edged the corners of his generous mouth and made his soft brown eyes light up almost impishly. One could easily imagine him gently bouncing a small child on one of his huge knees.

Mr. Simon began to round up the students. Miss

CAREERS IN THE HEALTH FIELD

Bard's candy-striped uniform was barely visible above the circle of excited, questioning, girls. Sandy Miles was escorting a small group around Faulkner Wing 8, and Henry held several young men entranced by the dramatic "live" stories that are characteristic of every hospital scene. "Ready, everyone?" Mr. Simon called. "We must move along to the operating room. If we hurry, we may be able to see an operation from the amphitheater." This news brought the students scurrying to his side.

The smell of anesthesia gases hung heavy in the long corridor as the group neared the amphitheater entrance. The excitement and the odor became too much for two girls, who asked to remain behind. However, the boys raced ahead and were already seated with the medical students when Mr. Simon entered. Over the intercom, the surgeon's voice could be heard explaining each step of the procedure. The high-intensity beams of light enveloped the green-garbed figures clustered around the table, giving them a soft but eerie glow. The nurses and interns were passing instruments to the surgeon while other nurses were assembling hot sterile pads and setting up additional instrument trays. Two *Operating Room Technicians* were assisting with equipment and machinery. There were nine people at work in the operation, yet, except for the steady, low announcements of the surgeon, the room was uneasily quiet. The figures seemed to move in pantomine fashion. The students

Live and in Color

whispered among themselves. Mr. Simon guessed their bewilderment. "The patient is a man who is having complicated intestinal surgery," the counselor explained. "I know it's hard to see much, but everything must be covered except the area being worked upon. You can see how smoothly they work together, each carrying out his responsibility."

"Where do *Operating Room Technicians* and *Surgical Technicians* get their education?" one of the boys inquired.

"They are trained here at the hospital. You can see how important it is for them to be calm, efficient and well organized." Mr. Simon replied.

"Boy, they move fast! I'd sure like to be one!" exclaimed the boy.

"Me too!" his obese friend chimed in.

"You need to lose 50 pounds first!" the first boy muttered scornfully.

"No matter, you'll both be able to talk with them after the surgery," Mr. Simon said, moving between them.

Dina and Bruce Knox, fraternal twins, lingered behind the group. They appeared to be discussing a matter of grave concern. Mr. Simon walked back to join them. "Is anything wrong?" the counselor asked.

"No—not really. Dina wants to see the artificial-kidney machine. Our brother Jonathan comes here to use it almost every week," Bruce revealed.

"I think we'll pass that department next." Mr. Simon's

right index finger traced the location on the hospital map. "Yes—it's just around the corner."

"Without a skilled technician to keep this valuable equipment in proper working condition, the machines would be idle half of the time. Our *Biomedical Equipment Technicians* are always on duty making minor repairs and servicing faulty instruments," Dr. Otto Price pointed out.

The students gathered around the complicated-looking machines. Dina reached out and touched a multi-gauged cabinet. "Is this what Jonathan uses to help his kidneys function?" she asked in a trembling voice.

"Yes—that's part of an artificial-kidney machine; the dialysis machine, which separates substances in solution, is over there." Dr. Price gestured toward the rear, where several students were talking with the technician. Dina and Bruce joined them as Harold, the technician, was describing his work.

"We work under the supervision of biomedical engineers. Our duties are to correct electronic devices, such as cardiac monitors (machines which permit the medical staff to observe the heart's performance) so that they function perfectly. If there are equipment problems, we check the machines, find the trouble and make the repairs." Harold demonstrated how the built-in alarms alerted the staff to malfunctioning. A loud, sirenlike screeching sound blasted from the machine.

Live and in Color

"What other machines can you fix?" a boy with curly, shoulder-length hair inquired.

"The heart-lung machine that is used in heart surgery, equipment for testing heart and lung function and machines which report blood pressure and brain waves during brain surgery," Harold answered.

"I like to build electronic gadgets and get good grades in math and science subjects. Does that mean I might be a good technician?" the student questioned further.

"Yes. I had a similar background before I earned a degree in mechanical technology from a two-year college."

Later, on the darkened bus, Mr. Simon sat alone listening to the students' comments as they incorporated the day's events into their own personal plans. Joking, laughing and shoving each other, they released built-up tensions. He thought to himself that some would be able to carry through projections for higher education, and others would find self-fulfillment in entry-level positions. But, most important, the opportunity for a promising career was available to each one.

Four ▶

THE THERAPIES

"I betcha it weighs more than 50 pounds!" Steve bragged to Ted Beams, *Physical Therapy Technician*.

"Not quite," Ted said. "It only seems that heavy." They were discussing Steve's cast, which was now a masterpiece of colorful designs, witty sayings, comic-strip figures and autographs. It would be a collector's item when removed; varnished, the cast would hang in a prominent place in Steve's room. Under the supervision of the chief therapist, Ted taught Steve exercises to strengthen his arm and shoulder muscles for crutch walking. The exercise program had begun while Steve was still hospitalized, and Steve had diligently carried out Ted's prescribed schedule at home. Several times a day, he went through the entire regimen. Steve was now able to manage the heavy cast when moving about his room. Today Ted planned to teach him how to take steps without putting weight on the injured leg.

The Therapies

"I missed you last week. Where were you?" Steve asked between pushups.

"I usually have Wednesdays off, because I have two classes that day at State," Ted replied.

"What are you studying?"

"I hope to be a *Rehabilitation Therapist* some day," Ted revealed.

Steve's face wore a puzzled look. "Don't you like your job?"

"Yes, I do—but as a rehabilitation therapist, I'll be able to help many more people. I'll be a generalist rather than a specialist. This means I can work with people who need help because of physical, mental, vocational, social, economic or cultural disabilities." Ted continued to count the pushups silently. "I can work most anywhere—mental hospitals, clinics, family or social agencies and even prisons. It's a new occupation in human services." Ted's voice rose in excitement.

"Sounds good, but doesn't it take years?" Steve asked.

Ted helped Steve roll over on the heavy mat before answering. "Not really. My A.A.S. [Associate in Applied Science] degree credits will count, and I'll take summer courses too." He walked Steve to the parallel bars. "Up and down the bars four times, and then you can rest. You've earned it!" Fondly, Ted dealt Steve a glancing blow to the chin and ambled over to a patient who was lifting weights attached to his ankle.

Steve completed his walking and stood in front of the

full-length mirror. "I'd swear that he's grown an inch since last month!" Glen Reade, the *Orthopedic Assistant,* observed. "Lean against the wall there while I get another pair." Glen pushed his long, tiered cart, and it spun around to display crutches, folded walkers, sandbags, pulleys, ropes, black iron discs of various weights, canvas back supports and a collection of hardware and small tools. He selected a pair of crutches, checked their length and passed them to Ted. "Try these for size," he said.

That spring afternoon when Dr. Jenkins visited State Training School for Boys had been a lucky day for Glen. Glen was ready for discharge from the reformatory, but he had nowhere to go. He volunteered to change a flat tire on the doctor's car. While he worked, they talked about Glen's plans. To return to the same neighborhood and its problems didn't seem practical to Dr. Jenkins, so he arranged for Glen to work at Tri-City. He began as a *Messenger*. Within six months, Glen requested a transfer to the rehabilitation department. As he made deliveries each day, he often took short cuts through that service and watched the therapists at work. Glen was deeply affected by the warmth, patience and tenderness demonstrated by the staff. He wanted to be a part of that group of dedicated humanitarians who brought hope to old, young, despondent and pain-creased faces. Mr. Welpin agreed to the transfer, and under the supervi-

The Therapies

sion of the staff Glen began the training immediately. For six months, he studied anatomy and physiology and learned how to apply and remove assistive and supportive devices, repair and adjust equipment and carry out preventive and therapeutic care programs. Dr. Jenkins referred Glen to one of the housing units of Tri-City; his trainee pay of $50 a week covered his moderate expenses. Glen loved his work. The staff became his family, the hospital his home.

Steve completed gait training with his new crutches, but he had a half-hour wait before the ambulance would pick him up. Ted held the wheelchair while Steve hoisted himself onto the seat. "My appointment is two weeks from today? OK. See you then!" Steve promised, and spun the wheels which sent him sailing down the hall. Ted gave a snappy salute and re-entered the ambulation room. Steve was looking for Jane Randall, the *Occupational Therapist Assistant* who had taught him how to make a beaded Indian headband. He brought the chair to an abrupt stop in front of the occupational therapy room. The sounds of frenzied activity spilled out beyond the closed doors. Steve heard the clamor of hammering, banging and scraping, mixed with shrill, excited voices. Sucking in a deep breath, he propelled the chair through the swinging doors.

The room had been transformed into a myriad of colored streamers, balloons and lights, and Steve frowned quizzically at the sight. "It's our annual bazaar, we sell the articles our patients have made during the year," Miss Randall explained. Steve swung aside to allow the workmen to continue with the booth they were constructing. A long table was piled high with brightly colored sweaters, mittens, furry toys, hooked rugs and embroidered bed and table linens. A woman wearing a prosthetic (artificial) arm was busy labeling sculpture, ceramic jewelry, stenciled metal belt buckles and crocheted baby booties. Across the room, a severely crippled arthritic man was shakily arranging watercolors, oils and collages on easels of varying heights. A flat tray placed across the arms of his wheelchair held picture frames done in needlepoint. "Steve, come look at this!" directed Miss Randall. "You remember Doris? See what she made." Steve saw a large tray which held a miniature farm scene complete with farmer, farmhouses and animals made with dyed pipe cleaners, bits of paper and cloth. Above the tray, suspended in mobile fashion, were cutouts in bright-green cardboard; they read "Farmer in the Dell."

Doris was 14 years old. Attempting to smother her flaming robe, set afire by a lighted cigarette, she had suffered severe burns of both hands.

"Doris did that? It's terrific!"

Miss Randall agreed. "Now you can see why I like this field of occupational therapy! Our prescribed arts and crafts serve as exercise to restore strength and motion to

The Therapies

muscles and joints. Making all these beautiful things also contributes to the mental and emotional adjustment of our patients."

Steve edged closer to examine a large collage of seashells. Miss Randall, carrying large bunches of artificial flowers, walked ahead, pushing aside chairs and stools to leave a path for Steve's chair. "We also teach handicapped patients daily living activities, such as cooking, housekeeping tasks and personal care."

"Do you need a license?" Steve wanted to know.

"No; but after high-school graduation and a course of 12 to 18 months, we are eligible for certification as occupational therapy assistants. Of course, we work under the supervision of a registered O.T. [occupational therapist]. The salary's not bad either; I make about $130 for a 37-hour week." Miss Randall arranged the multicolored flowers in tall blue-green vases on the beige-colored cloth covering a long table.

Two workmen were attaching a small chair to a four-foot-high platform; another was fitting a red satin-lined canopy to the chair. "That looks like a throne!" Steve said with a puzzled tone in his voice.

"That's exactly what it is," boomed a voice from the back of the room. "A throne for the princess of our bazaar." Steve pivoted his chair. A tall man was weaving his way toward them. He held a tiny, pig-tailed girl, sleepily cradled in his arms. Steve recognized Daniel, the *Orthotist*, who made and fitted braces. "How are you coming along, Steve?" he asked.

CAREERS IN THE HEALTH FIELD

"I'm doing OK, thanks. Is the throne for her?" Steve asked.

"Yes. It is. Meet our girl Jennifer Stokes—better known around here as 'Princess Jenny.' You can give her a ride while we check on her throne." Daniel gently placed the young girl in Steve's lap. Jenny gave Steve a half-smile and snuggled deeper into his navy pea jacket. Jenny's long princess gown and cloak hid the heavy spinal and leg braces, but the cold steel pressing against Steve's body was stabbing evidence of their presence.

"Let's roll!" Steve blushed at the shrillness of his own voice; his throat was tight with unshed tears. The chair whirled forward, and Jenny squealed with excitement, tightening her grip on Steve's forearms. Daniel and Miss Randall watched from a safe distance, joined by Earl Sedgwick.

Earl, the department's *Prosthetic Assistant,* and Daniel had known each other at the local community college. After completing two years of formal study, they received four years of supervised work and instruction from the staff at Tri-City. Both were now certified through their professional association, the American Orthotic and Prosthetics Association. Earl and Daniel had chosen hospital work, although many opportunities were available to them in homes for the aged, veteran's hospitals and surgical appliance stores. They often worked together when fitting artificial limbs and braces and instructing patients

The Therapies

in their use. Their specialties, closely related, are carried out only with the physician's prescription.

"Is Steve Bowman here?" It was the volunteer driver of the ambulance. "Come on—we're waiting," he called from the hallway. Jenny was still flushed from her thrilling ride. She waved good-bye to Steve from her throne.

"She fits it perfectly," Steve observed as he went through the doors.

Jane Randall had worked steadily for two hours; now she stood back and surveyed the occupational therapy room. It did look like a scene from a fairy tale. All the pretty things! Sales would double the last year's! She was tired but happy; tonight she and Kirby were shopping for bedroom furniture. Jane glanced at her watch. Kirby would be finished in another hour. She pulled off her pink smock, flipped the switch and quickly locked the door. The thought of seeing Kirby made all those tired feelings vanish.

Radiology is a growing branch of medicine concerned with the use of x-rays and other forms of ionizing radiation as aids in diagnosis and treatment. A radiologist works in the areas of nuclear medicine and radiation therapy. Kirby Belding was such a technologist. When he successfully passed two certification examinations of the American Registry of Radiological Technologists, he became a *Radiological Technologist* (R.T.) and was certified in the areas of nuclear medicine and radiation therapy. Kirby had learned about such things as isotopes while still in high school. During his freshman year, his grandmother's illness was diagnosed as malignant. Surgical procedures had been used before the long series of radiation treatments were recommended by her doctors. Five times a week, Kirby accompanied his grandmother to the radiotherapy department of Tri-City Hospital. These visits were his first exposure to ill people and his first realization that cancer affected persons of all age groups. During those months, he witnessed heartbreak and joy in equal amounts. He glimpsed equipment that was akin to that in his science fiction magazines. More important, he began to identify with his grandmother's therapist, Jason Reuben. Mr. Reuben carefully explained how the impressive and sophisticated machinery was helping to rid his grandmother of the dreaded disease. After clinic hours, Kirby was given an escorted tour of the department; Mr. Reuben allowed him to enter the therapy rooms and get a closer look at all that powerful equipment. Kirby attended a physics lecture with students who were completing their clinic affiliation. But, in the end, it was Mr. Reuben himself who influenced Kirby the most. Mr. Reuben was sympathetic but objective, kind but firm and always accurate and precise in carrying out the treatment program. Kirby was pleased to learn that high grades in mathematics and science, his two best subjects, were important as a basis for the required two years or more of study beyond high

The Therapies

school. Mr. Reuben advised him of a school approved by the American Medical Association, and Kirby entered a two-year program of hospital training and classroom work. After he received an Associate Degree in Applied Science (A.A.S.), he took additional courses in radiation physics, radiation biology, radioisotopes, chemistry and atomic physics, coupled with supervised clinical experience for another year. Kirby now attended evening courses at State and hoped to earn a bachelor's degree soon; his early aptitude in science had led to a choice of physics as his major field of concentration. His friendship with Mr. Reuben had continued over the years, and he had eventually come to Tri-City. Mr. Reuben, now a supervisor, had not only hired him but introduced him to Jane!

Jane and Mr. Reuben were watching Kirby position a patient on the treatment hammock. Kirby carefully measured off the area to be treated; he checked his calculations several times. He had to be certain that only the affected area received the powerful dose of radiation. Satisfied that his measurements were exact and that the patient's position on the table provided safety and comfort, Kirby swung closed the heavy doors to the treatment chamber. From his stool facing the countless control dials, Kirby watched through the glass-paned porthole while he administered the treatment. The patient was under his critical observation every second.

CAREERS IN THE HEALTH FIELD

"Where are you kids off to?" Mr. Reuben was helping Kirby complete his daily treatment records. The patients had left, and the rooms were strangely quiet. "We're shopping again," volunteered Jane.

Kirby helped Jane into her coat, and they strolled arm in arm toward the outer door, turning once to wave good-bye to Mr. Reuben.

Five ▶

SOS.........

"Code 3: Go to Emergency Room 2! Code 3: Go to Emergency Room 2! Repeat . . . Code 3: Emergency Room 2!" The command shrieked over the loudspeaker; its military precision partially masked tremors of controlled emotion. To the staff of Tri-City Hospital, the words were ominous. Someone was in serious trouble; someone was dying!

A cardiac resident, eating lunch, dropped his fork from midair and sprinted from the cafeteria. Two residents on rounds quickly covered their patients and raced toward the elevator. Elevator #3 had discharged the passengers and soared to the fourth floor at the first alert. Morris, the operator, knew that special equipment used in a Code 3 alert would be waiting there. He brought his car to a jarring stop and shoved open the doors. An orderlie pushed in the carts holding the monitor, resuscitator and defibrillator machines (special equipment used in an attempt to restore consciousness). Morris almost slammed the door on the two hurrying residents as he sped to the main floor; the repeated buzzing of the prearranged signal there meant that the nursing supervisor, Lynnette Moore, was responding to the alert. She jumped in as the car paused momentarily in its race to the basement. Before the doors were completely opened, hands reached into the car and grabbed for the equipment. The residents and supervisor squeezed by and joined the medley of flying white shoes, caps and jackets racing to get there in time.

The treatment room was crowded with staff and equipment. The cardiac resident was pounding the patient's chest, an oxygen mask covered his face, and heart stimulants were being injected into the veins of his right arm. "Speed up the I.V. [intravenous fluids], nurse! Raise his head a little higher! Any blood pressure yet?"

"No pulse! Got a faint heartbeat!" the medical resident cried, moving the stethescope over the chest.

"Good, but he's not out of it yet. Let's get to work!" Orders for drugs, tests and treatments cracked sharply through the now quiet room. John Doe, struck down by American's No. 1 killer, had apparently survived his first heart attack!

This dramatic episode may be repeated several times a day in hospitals everywhere. In some instances, the voice booms throughout the institution, shouting "Red Alert" or "Red Blanket"; in other places, it may cry out "Team

SOS ··· _ _ _ ···

700." Whatever the words, the meaning is clear. Someone is in need of expert emergency care! Sometimes the first response to the call for help comes from a volunteer team of skilled ambulance and rescue corpsmen. But with increasing frequency, the *Medical Emergency Technician* is first on the scene. You'll recall that it was Jim Fields, a senior technician, who responded to Steve Bowman's call for help earlier in our story.

Jim Fields and his family moved into a large housing development on the edge of town. Although the development provided housing for more than 3,000 people, the nearest hospital was more than six miles away. During the first year Jim lived there, several people had long waits for the ambulance's arrival. These were terrifying experiences for the patient and his family. One night, at a tenants' council meeting, a proposal was made to recruit and train ambulance and rescue corpsmen. Jim was among the first to volunteer. "Who will provide the training?" he asked.

"The over-all program will be administered by a physician, but he'll bring in specialists as needed. For example, has anyone here ever delivered a baby?" the council leader wanted to know. His response was a chorous of noes.

Dr. Martin Schuler presided at the first meeting of the 18 volunteers. "Let's see. We have a nurses' aide, two housewives, three teachers, a grocery clerk, an accountant, a salesman, a graduate student, a minister, a chef,

CAREERS IN THE HEALTH FIELD

two secretaries, two mechanics, a bus driver and a pharmacist! A good balance," he observed. "Age range is fine too, from 22 to 55 years. Most important, is everyone in the best of health? I'll need a report of a recent physical examination from each of you."

In 20 biweekly training sessions, the 15 corps members (three were disqualified for health reasons) learned skills and techniques to be used in cases of medical emergency. Specialists in related medical areas taught them how to deliver babies; restrain mentally disturbed persons; render first aid for burns, drug overdoses, hemorrhages and heart attacks; perform resuscitation (restore breathing); and many other important procedures. Jim Fields never missed a session; he was assigned to Squad #1, but he often voluntarily joined the other squads. "You spend all your time with that emergency unit! Why don't you work at it full time?" his wife complained late one night. The next day Jim Fields walked into Mr. Welpin's office. Because of his previous experience and training, Jim was immediately assigned to ambulance duty. His supervisor recognized Jim's potential for assuming a more responsible role in the department and recommended that he receive formal instruction at a two-year college. Jim worked hard and did well in such courses as biology, chemistry, anatomy and physiology, psychology and sociology. He was permitted to complete his field-work requirements at Tri-City while on the job. Jim received intensive instruction in all areas of emergency care. After two years, he earned an A.A.S. (Associate in Applied Science) degree and became a licensed emergency medical technician. (This license is available in some states and required in others.) Because Jim's training was so thorough, he qualified to take the examination for the registered nurse license. As his supervisor predicted, Jim was promoted to senior technician and earned $180 a week in his first year.

"Do we have a bed in C.C.U. [coronary care unit]? I'd like our John Doe to spend a few days up there. He still needs continuous observation." The Code 3 team had completed the emergency care, and the patient could now be moved. Within minutes, with bottles swinging from poles attached to the stretcher, the cardiac resident and orderlies quickly maneuvered the stretcher and the portable oxygen unit into the waiting elevator. "Morris —C.C.U. on the double, please!"

"Bed No. 2 is ready, Dr. Pryor. We have a name now. He's a Mr. Craig Tulane," the charge nurse said, circling a plastic name band around the patient's left wrist. Dr. Pryor carefully attached and checked the tubing to the complicated and impressive array of machinery above the head of Mr. Tulane's bed. "Let's review the orders," he said to the charge nurse. "Barney is assigned to this unit; I'll call him."

Barney Jaffee was a *Cardiopulmonary Technician;* he performed a wide range of tasks related to the function and therapeutic care of the heart-lung system. He had

CAREERS IN THE HEALTH FIELD

been trained to perform a variety of tests for measuring the body's production and consumption of energy. Barney often assisted the doctors with intricate heart examination and tests done in the operating room. Now he would be responsible for observing and recording the messages sent from Mr. Tulane's body and flashed across the monitor screens. In an emergency situation, the doctors and nurses would be nearby to give him instructions and supervision. Barney and two other technicians were participating in a pilot project which required the use of paramedical technicians in intensive-care units. The study hoped to demonstrate that much of the skilled care of patients in recovery and intensive-care units can be entrusted to properly trained paramedical people. They must function in relatively narrow fields, but good basic and practical training prepares them to do routine and emergency procedures. For example, if necessary, Barney could operate a respirator or assist the doctor with tracheal intubation. (A tube is inserted into the throat to permit the flow of air to the lungs.) The three technicians were high-school graduates with high scores in manual dexterity. Each had hoped for some kind of medical career but had been unable to afford formal education. Their assignment to the C.C.U. had provided an opportunity for them to explore their interests and talents in a most satisfying way.

"I'll be finished here in a minute, Barney, and we can go to lunch together."

"OK, I'll wait."

The *Biomedical Equipment Assistant* was running his final check on the monitoring devices attached to Mr. Tulane's chest, arms and legs. He usually spent two hours every week in the C.C.U., inspecting, adjusting and maintaining every piece of equipment in perfect working order. When necessary, he made minimal repairs. Harvey, the repairman, was also qualified to make simple repairs on equipment used elsewhere in the hospital. For example, he routinely inspected electrocardiograph and encephalograph machines, intricate and delicate instruments used in x-ray and surgical tools. When it was necessary, he consulted with Harold, the *Biomedical Engineering Technician* assigned to the operating room, on complicated and detailed repairs or adjustments. Harvey had attended a vocational high school, where he studied electrical installation techniques. After graduation, he entered a community college and earned an associate degree in applied science in electrical technology. Harvey's courses there included subjects like electrical circuit analysis, electronics, feedback control systems and communication and microwave electronics. Laboratory courses featuring the lastest equipment and procedures were important to the degree requirements. He began at Tri-City Hospital as a technical assistant to the hospital's engineering crew, and after one year was promoted to instrument repair and maintenance. Harvey tightened the last screw and called out to Barney, "I'm done here—let's go. I'm very hungry."

"Nurse, will you please telephone for a portable chest x-ray to be done on Mr. Tulane. I'll make out the request forms now." Dr. Pryor spent a great deal of time on C.C.U. attending to the critically ill patients there. He would wait for the x-ray technologist and assist him in positioning the patient. X-rays, a common tool of modern medicine, permit the physician to obtain pictures of the body's bones and inner organs. As part of the radiology team, the x-ray technologist plays a vital role. To become one requires certain aptitudes. Because he deals directly with patients, it is important that this technologist be gentle and sympathetic. He must also be skillful with his hands and intelligent about the machinery and other equipment he uses. A natural ability in scientific subjects in high school is important; the job demands the utmost accuracy and care, since errors may be dangerous to the patient. Technologists process film in the darkroom, assist radiologists (physicians who specialize in radiology and interpret the x-ray pictures) in fluoroscopy and perform many other duties related to the x-ray examination. This field offers excellent opportunities for someone who would like to work in a professional atmosphere, but who, for whatever reason, can't spend more than two years on post–high-school work. While in high school, one should take general science, biology, chemistry and physics, coupled with a solid background in mathematics. Most approved schools are found in hospitals, community colleges and medical schools; they offer a two-year training program of formal study and field experience. Graduates of schools approved by the American Medical Association are eligible to take a certification examination offered by the American Registry of Radiological Technologists in X-Ray. If one passes, he is certified as a registered technologist in x-ray and may use the initials R.T. after his name. Such certification is a requirement for employment in many hospitals. Like Kirby, the nuclear medicine and radiation technologist, an x-ray technologist may apply for membership in the American Society of Radiology Technologists. This society cooperates with the American College of Radiology and the American Registry of Radiological Technologists in maintaining high educational standards and professional stature. Although one-third of all technologists are employed by hospitals, they may work in local and state departments of public health, in physicians' offices or clinics and in industrial plants. Part-time, night and rotating shifts are routinely offered in large hospitals; this arrangement attracts women who want to combine career with marriage and child care. Salaries begin at $5,500 a year in general, but with experience and increased skill, a technologist may advance to $12,000 a year.

"What's the special for today?" Barney asked the counter

girl. Harvey grabbed a tray and joined Barney on the slow-moving line in front of the counter.

"There's Cory in the corner. Let's sit with him," Barney suggested.

Cory was an *Inhalation Therapist*. He had supplied the vital oxygen therapy in the emergency care of Mr. Tulane. Cory's occupation, a new allied health science profession, is one that is expanding rapidly. The goal of inhalation therapy is to make sure that the human body is receiving an adequate supply of oxygen and, at the same time, getting rid of carbon dioxide. The inhalation therapy specialist is a very important member of the health team. Without oxygen, brain tissue begins to die in four minutes and the heart will stop in nine. Cory always followed the physician's recommendations when assembling and applying respiratory equipment. His courses had provided sufficient knowledge of the chemistry and pharmacology of the drugs administered with the oxygen. Cory was frequently called upon to instruct patients in the use of special equipment; he was tactful, gentle and understanding of their emotional distress. Each spring, he conducted a seminar for interns and student nurses at which he demonstrated the technical operation of his equipment and the application of various techniques to specific illness. Cory utilized proper aseptic procedures in patient care by cleaning and sterilizing each piece of equipment used by the patients. Because much of this technician's services are rendered in emergency situations, all of his equipment must be in top working order; if necessary, he must be prepared to make repairs on the spot. A malfunction could be fatal!

Hospitals are the largest employers of inhalation therapists. In some institutions, they may aid in the diagnosis of respiratory diseases by performing important blood tests for the doctor. They may also analyze blood samples to learn how the oxygen therapy affects the patients. Cory earned his A.A.S. (Associate in Applied Science) degree concurrently with his inhalation therapy training from an allied health college of a large university. This training is available in community colleges and large teaching hospitals. Cory passed the national certification examination of the American Registry of Inhalation Therapists. He was qualified to use the initials R.I.T. (registered inhalation therapist) after his name.

Soon Barney, Harvey and Cory were joined by their friend Vance, a *Pharmacy Technician*. He was a member of one of the emerging occupations that can be found in many large hospitals. Vance assisted the staff of three licensed pharmacists of Tri-City Hospital in a variety of ways. He prepared routine stock drugs and solutions for hospital use. In an emergency, he personally delivered the drugs to the operating room or emergency room. At times, a prescription had to be filled outside the hospital, because the drug was rarely prescribed. Vance would bring the much-needed medication directly to the floor.

CAREERS IN THE HEALTH FIELD

His other duties included assisting the pharmacists in dispensing drugs, packaging drugs for home use, preparing inventories and storing pharmaceuticals. More than 500 new drug products are placed on the market each year. This places a great deal of responsibility upon the modern pharmacists, because the physician expects them to know all about drugs and medications, old or new. Of all the drugs prescribed today, more than one-half were unheard of before World War II. The pharmacist faces a continuing challenge to keep abreast of the new products of scientific research. Vance and others like him help provide the pharmacist with time to spend in studying new additions to the drug market.

A pharmacy technician can assist the pharmacist in a neighborhood drug store. Here he may dispense factory-made products. Working under the supervision of a licensed pharmacist, he can help prepare the combination of drugs often required to fill a prescription. Other employment possibilities exist in pharmaceutical companies, where the technician may assist the scientists who discover, develop, manufacture and maintain quality control for new products. Additional opportunities may be found in public health, the Veterans' Administration and large public and private institutions, such as mental hospitals, homes for the aged and prisons.

Vance had pursued a college preparatory course while in high school, because he had dreams of becoming a pharmacist. Family financial difficulties altered his plans, so Vance enlisted in the U.S. Navy. His experience as pharmacist mate prepared him for his present position. However, he could have received on-the-job training without armed services background. His salary was $125 a week, but with more experience and some formal study, he could receive periodic raises.

Six ▶

ROOM AND BOARD

"Faulkner Wing 8, Miss Holt speaking! Just a minute, please. Mr. Fulton! Mr. Fulton! How many discharges for today? Thanks, I'll tell her." Miss Holt, day *Unit Clerk,* returned to the telephone. "Hello . . . Housekeeping? Mr. Fulton says we have four for this morning and one after lunch." Miss Holt replaced the telephone on its cradle and stretched across the desk to the chart rack. "Garcia, Alcott, Eldridge, Goldin and Spitzer. Is Mrs. Eldridge the one leaving after lunch?"

"Yes. The others are all signed out."

Miss Holt removed the five charts from the rack. Discarding the protective metal covers, she dismantled each chart and replaced the varied colored sheets in the order prescribed by the record room.

Rooms 12 and 17 were vacant; Mrs. Bella Rohan was supervising the "check out" staff. Mrs. Rohan had been *Executive Housekeeper* at Tri-City for over four years and was currently earning $19,000 a year. This position followed a series of incidents, starting with her emergency surgery. During her hospitalization, the Tremont Hotel, her employers, instituted bankruptcy proceedings. By a lucky coincidence, the position of executive housekeeper became available at Tri-City Hospital.

Similarities exist in all institutional housekeeping, whether it takes place in a hospital, hotel or home for the aged. Each houses a number of persons who must be fed, have comfortable attractive quarters and live in a clean, sanitary environment. As in her former hotel position of administrator of housekeeping services, Mrs. Rohan was primarily an administrator and supervisor who directed the whole hospital program through area housekeepers, who supervised the work of employees in their areas. Mrs. Rohan often came up to the floors to observe her staff at work; many were graduates of the training program introduced by her for new employees.

"I think those yellow-striped drapes go beautifully with the soft blue of the walls." Mrs. Rohan and the *Area Supervisor* were standing in the doorway of the newly "clean" room 12. It was not accidental that the room's furnishings were attractively correlated. Mrs. Rohan had a flair for color and design. She had worked closely with the staff of a professional decorating firm who designed, selected or bought all the furnishings and fixtures for the patients' rooms, visitors' and staff lounges, pediatric and obstetric suites and cafeterias. As a teenager, she had designed and made her own clothes, and after high-school graduation, she even spent a year at a fashion institute. But, like many young people, Mrs. Rohan did not find fulfillment in her first career choice, and switched first to business administration and later to secretarial courses. By the time she was 24 years old, Mrs. Rohan had worked as a secretary, clerk, junior accountant, saleslady and window dresser; meanwhile, she completed evening courses for a degree in home economics. All of this provided an excellent background for her first institutional position—as housekeeper in a small motel. Her duties included supervision of all housekeeping personnel, management of linen supplies and purchasing of supplies and equipment. Mrs. Rohan's ability to sustain a high level of performance in the staff, create harmonious interpersonal relationships and produce a profit for the owners earned her a promotion to executive housekeeper for the large Tremont Hotel.

All five rooms were spotlessly clean and ready for the new patients. The area supervisor and her staff of two *Maids,* a *General Cleaner* and a *Floor Waxer* had joined forces in putting the rooms in order. This staff, attractively dressed in gray uniforms and white shoes, wore protective latex gloves as they worked. The maids washed the beds and plastic-covered mattresses and made the beds with fresh linens. Bedside and over-the-bed tables, flower stands and vinyl-covered furniture were soaped down and rinsed with antiseptic-laden water. Meanwhile, the cleaning man scoured the tiles around the sink and toilet

Room and Board

areas, washed the window sills and scrubbed the floors. Sterilized and plastic-wrapped personal articles, such as basins, disposable pitchers and drinking glasses, bedpans and urinals, were placed in their proper places in the stands. Paper towels, paper cups, soap and new thermometers were left in each room. The floor waxer was last, as usual; he added the finishing touch—a sparkling, nonskid floor.

"Have you finished your evaluations of the staff?" Mrs. Rohan asked when she and the area supervisor returned to the ward manager's office.

"Yes. Shall we review them?" The supervisor pulled two chairs nearer to the desk, smoothed out her white skirt and sat down. She opened a loose-leaf notebook and began. "Mrs. Childs has perfect attendance, always completes her work on time and can be depended upon to do a thorough job. Miss Rivera is still attending evening classes, but should have her diploma by June. She works well with the rest of the staff, and once her English is perfected, she will be considered for a more responsible assignment. Mr. Peoples, our floor waxer, suggested a different kind of wax—one with a harder finish. He's neat and courteous and he keeps his machines in good working order. Our general cleaner, Mr. Gabriel, takes a longer lunch hour than he should, but he's got a wonderful sense of humor. They're really a fine crew; your training program appears to be successful."

Mrs. Rohan had developed an orientation program

for new housekeeping personnel; the courses included training in cleaning techniques which allowed for infection control, safety measures for the employees and sanitary disposal of refuse. All maids, porters, cleaners, linen room handlers and laundry workers took this training. After experience, men and women from this group were eligible for consideration for the post of area supervisor. Mrs. Rohan gathered up the evaluations and stood up, ending the conference. "Things are going well here; you're doing a good job! I must go down to the laundry, before I meet with the chef. Are you going to our Ten-Year Awards Banquet?" The area supervisor assured Mrs. Rohan that she was.

The laundry was a beehive of activity, a far cry from the steaming-hot, medieval dungeon of old. New equipment and machinery, air conditioning, fluorescent lighting, brightly colored painted walls and furniture and the soft hum of piped-in music had converted it into a most pleasant environment. The new equipment required less staff, but demanded new and different skills of the workers. For example, the new wash-and-wear fabrics needed particular handling in regard to bleaching and ironing. The bed linens, towels and patients' shirts and drapes were separated before washing from gowns, towels, sheets and covers used by hospital services by the *Sorters*. All flat items were machine-folded as they came from the extractors; they were then placed in warming bins for complete drying. The *Assistant Super-*

visor was moving among the machines observing the *Washers, Pullers* and *Extractors*. These were the main production people, who held entry-level positions averaging $98 for a 35-hour week. Across the room, the *Assistant Manager* was making a final check of the linen trucks before their delivery to the floors.

"Two blankets and 15 washcloths missing from this one, but the next one's ready to go." He was speaking to the *Packers*, who were responsible for loading the trucks according to the linen request sheets the ward managers submitted each day. When all the trucks were delivered, the *Linen Room Handlers* would sort the excesses into neat piles on shelves in the linen room. "Oh, hello!" greeted the assistant manager as Mrs. Rohan approached. "Come to visit Jana?"

"Yes! I want to try out these large gripper snaps on the children's shirts and pajamas. They're attractive and will encourage the little ones to dress themselves."

Jana was a talented dressmaker; until her accident, she had worked for a leading designer of women's clothes. Now, from a wheelchair, she supervised a staff of three women who did all the mending, repairing and alterations for the hospital. For instance, they sewed bed and table linens, draperies, screen covers, uniforms and lab coats. These *Seamstresses* were all experienced former factory workers, but seasonal employment forced them to seek work with more security. Jana, the *Head Seamstress,* and her staff occupied a sunny room adjacent to the laundry. Mrs. Rohan and Jana frequently collaborated on ideas for decorating or designing furnishings or clothing. It was Jana who designed and made the sample for the attractive green jumpsuits worn by the doctors and nurses in the operating room suites. Jana also sketched the pattern for the pink and blue culottes seen on the nurses and aides assigned to pediatrics. From her wheelchair, she cut her patterns and sewed her samples. No one ever considered Jana handicapped. Her $170 a week salary had paid for the small car that she drove to work each day.

Mrs. Rohan hurried past the cafeterias and coffee shop on the way to her appointment with chef Wendell Williams and administrative dietitian Florence Young. They were planning to make final arrangements for the annual Ten-Year Awards Banquet given each year to honor employees with ten years of service. Today they must decide on the menu, seating plans and table decorations. This was a busy hour in the vast kitchen; hundreds of supper trays with a variety of menus had to be ready for 5:30 P.M. supper. Mrs. Rohan paused at the kitchen's main entrance and watched the kitchen staff at work—a complex of stations or centers under a galaxy of lights. There were the *Broiler Cooks, Vegetable* and *Soup Cooks, Pastry Cooks, Salad Men* and *General Food Handlers.* Down the center of the kitchen, three waist-high conveyor belts were inching along. *Diet Aides,* smartly

Room and Board

dressed in yellow and white checkered uniforms with matching headbands, stood at strategic points along the way. Partially set with silver, condiments and beverages, the patients' trays slowly moved before the aides. Each tray carried several plastic disks of assorted colors; these had been added earlier by a team of aides to indicate the food selections made by patients. A large chart, hung over the counter, explained that a green disk meant salad, a red stood for meat, white for fish, blue for soup, etc. As the trays made the trip down the conveyor belts, an aide substituted an appropriate food for a disk.

The *Dietary Technicians* sat on stools at the ends of the long counters; their clip boards held the patients' menus. With an experienced eye, the technicians quickly checked the trays for accuracy in special diets, neatness and appetite appeal. Occasionally a garnish of lemon slice, parsley or pimiento was added or a food substitution made; every effort was extended to stimulate the diminished appetites of most of the patients. The trays were quickly loaded into insulated food trucks by the general food handlers. Each truck held 32 trays; when three trucks were filled and coupled together, they were attached to a motorized carrier, which sped them to the freight elevators and then to the appropriate floors. Diet aides awaited them there, and quickly extracted the trays and served them under the supervision of a dietary technician. The whole operation demonstrated how well

CAREERS IN THE HEALTH FIELD

people with various levels of skills and responsibilities can work together under able administration and supervision.

Mrs. Florence Young, *Administrative Dietitian,* provided such administrative leadership. She was responsible for large-scale meal planning and preparation and purchasing foods and supplies, as well as training personnel. Mrs. Young once revealed that her interest in this field began because she had a weight problem. Fad and starvation diets left her temporarily slim but listless. In desperation, she decided to learn more about low-calorie foods which were also nutritious. She experimented and adapted recipes and menus to suit her needs and sensibly lost a great deal of weight. Mrs. Young's physician admired her self-discipline and perseverance; he encouraged her to enter the field and help others live healthier lives through better nutrition. After receiving a baccalaureate degree, she served a one-year internship in food service administration. Mrs. Young qualified for positions in the Armed Forces, university and college food services, business and industry and public school programs, but chose the hospital position because it presented an opportunity to teach. In spite of a heavy schedule, she managed to design and conduct courses for nursing, medical and dental students, patients and their families and community groups. Besides four dietitians, her staff included 20 graduates of two-year college programs in dietetics, employed as dietary technicians at salaries averaging $150 a week. Mrs. Young had trained them to carry out the day-to-day operations, such as preparing and serving meals under safe and sanitary conditions, ordering food, keeping food cost records and taking an inventory of supplies and equipment. The 40 diet aides' duties covered the whole range of food preparation, storing and serving and the care and cleaning of facilities. Their training was completed in four months. With prior experience in food preparation or service, these men and women could receive weekly paychecks of $98 to $115.

"Hope I'm not late, but every time I pass that assembly-line performance in the kitchen, I have to stop and admire it."

Mrs. Young poured a cup of coffee for Mrs. Rohan and made room for her on the settee. "Wendell and I were going through files checking menus of previous banquets. Heaven help us if we serve the same menu two years in a row! Wendell has some ideas about doing things a little differently this year."

Wendell Williams was *Executive Chef* and had complete responsibility for seeing that the menus so carefully planned by the dietary staff were turned into mouthwatering meals. He particularly enjoyed participating in the Chefs and Cooks Union program for training *Apprentice Cooks* and *Salad Men;* these were usually young men recently out of high school who wanted training combined with employment. During their first three months, apprentices learned the fundamental principles of professional cooking and received a basic introduction to food service and the related areas. These young men spent ten hours a week in classroom study. They learned to identify and know foods, including raw, cooked and prepared forms, cuts of meat and the like; they also had to know their uses, seasons, market and quality factors. The trainees were expected to be familiar with basic principles of nutrition, sanitation, hygiene, food handling, storage and preservation, heat and refrigeration, as well as principles and procedures in dish and pot washing.

During the next three months, the apprentices learned about the financial and economic basis of the industry. They became familiar with balance sheets, budgets, operating statements, recipe and menu precosting and food and beverage cost controls. The final weeks included instruction in table service and dining room operation, baking, institutional feeding and management. Through classes and practical experience, these future chefs developed some basic understanding of human relations in dealing with people, personnel problems and labor relations. Young men accepted for the program were expected to be able to read, use and adapt recipes. Other personal qualifications for potential cooks and chefs include well developed eye-hand coordination, motion deftness, agility and tool skills. A feeling for creativity, color and design are also important aptitudes.

Room and Board

The food service industry, one of the country's largest industries in dollar sales and number of people employed, is assured of continued growth with increased travel, the expansion of hotels and motels and the continuing demands of industry. The greatest single need of the industry is for trained cooks, chefs and related service personnel. Salaries are usually equated with skills, experience and type of facility: a short-order cook in a luncheonette may earn $6,500 a year, whereas an executive chef in a first-class or luxury hotel may earn as much as $32,000 annually.

Wendell's plan for the banquet involved the apprentices. The chef put down his cup and turned to his notes. "I'd like to give my boys a chance to really show what they can do. Pedro, Wally and Tony have been here for nine months and are about ready to go out on their own. We could use three entrees; each apprentice cook can make his specialty."

"That's a splendid idea!" Mrs. Young commented enthusiastically. "What will they make?"

Wendell searched his notes. "Pedro can do a delicious veal scallopine with Marsala wine. Wally is great with his Pompano Almondine. Tony has an original dish made with boned breast of chicken, mushrooms and parmesan cheese."

Both women, wearing pensive expressions, were listening attentively. "We'll probably ruin the budget, but let's do it anyway," Mrs. Young finally said.

CAREERS IN THE HEALTH FIELD

Mrs. Rohan was excitedly jotting down ideas on her pad. "I agree. Let's plan on 200 people attending. We'll seat them at 20 round tables. I've always felt that those long tables are cold and unfriendly. Each table will have a host or hostess, and we'll seat an equal number of award winners at each table."

Mrs. Young was also busy making notes, but looked up to ask, "How does this strike you? My dietary technicians are dying to show off too! They could plan a different but coordinated theme for each table. For instance, each table could symbolically represent a different department of the hospital. We still have that handsome stork the girls made for Lillian's baby shower. It would make a beautiful centerpiece. We could enlist the aid of that pretty young Jane Randall in the occupational therapy room; she's very talented, I hear."

Wendell was still checking the menus of past banquets. "Well, it will be the first time we ever offered three entrees! I suggest that we avoid such routine things as peas and carrots, if it's all right with you two. One of my apprentice salad men has an unusual apple slaw that would go well with Tony's chicken."

Mrs. Young and Mrs. Rohan were discussing such things as carnation pink table cloths and brown linen napkins. Mrs. Rohan had several suggestions for using lots of fresh green leaves and early spring flowers. Mrs. Young turned as Wendell got up to leave. "I think this year's banquet will be the best yet—but please remember us poor dieters, Wendell. Could you at least plan on a little low-calorie sherbet?"

Seven ▶

KEEPING THE RECORD STRAIGHT

"How many are coming? I'll order coffee and pastry now. It's an important meeting; I think everyone will attend." Mr. Charles Boothe was discussing the monthly meeting of the Educational Council with his secretary. As principal of Aldrich High School, Mr. Boothe was supposed to convene the meetings of the Educational Council, whose members were representatives of local business and industry and health, social and welfare agencies. The organization worked toward broadening and improving students' educational and social experiences.

"What is today's topic?" The secretary was placing lined pads and pencils along the long board-room table.

"We're about to begin our first venture into Cooperative Education. The people from Tri-City Hospital will outline the plan this morning."

The meeting began at 9:30 A.M. As Mr. Boothe predicted, all 15 members were present. The principal explained that "cooperative education" proposes that well-educated individuals can best be developed through an educational pattern which periodically provides exposure to the world of work. It is "cooperative" in that it is dependent upon the cooperation of educators and employers to jointly design a superior total educational program.

"How does it differ from part-time jobs?" a plastics firm manager wanted to know.

"This program has an interrelated work and study content, planned and supervised by teachers and employers. It's been successful in many high schools. Suppose we let Mr. Stanton from Tri-City present his proposal." Mr. Boothe nodded in the direction of an athletic-looking, blond man wearing steel-rimmed glasses.

Mr. Stanton shifted his chair so that he faced most of the men and women seated at the table. "We're prepared to offer students real jobs performed under actual working conditions; based on merit, the students can even earn advancements. Because of our need for skilled office and secretarial assistance and Aldrich High's large and reputable business education and secretarial sciences departments, we will begin with positions requiring these talents. Tri-City needs medical transcribers, medical secretaries, programmers, typist/clerks, unit clerks, stenographers and general office clerks."

A man from a baking firm raised his hand. "Will all seniors be required to be "cooperatives?"

"Oh, no! It's all voluntary."

CAREERS IN THE HEALTH FIELD

"It sounds expensive to me. I mean . . . as a businessman."

Mr. Stanton handed him a sheet of paper from an attaché case. "You'll see that it's really an investment that works two ways: the students receive supervised, paid working experience, and Tri-City has an opportunity to build competent staff around a nucleus of well-trained young people." Pointing to a diagram on the paper, Mr. Stanton said: "See how education, training and supervision are shared by the school and the hospital!"

The man appeared satisfied, but a female social investigator asked about the real values of such a program. Mr. Stanton reassured her. "Most research has been done on programs in colleges, but the results appear to apply to 17-to-19-year-old high-school seniors too. Results indicate that students find greater meaning in their courses, their motivation for academic pursuit is increased and they develop greater skills in human relations."

The group quietly read the assorted papers passed to them by Mr. Stanton. Mr. Boothe looked toward the wall clock and suggested, "Let's take a short break. Mr. Kurt Simon, the seniors' guidance counselor, and teachers involved in the cooperative plan will join us shortly to present additional information for discussion."

Mrs. Lyndon hurried into the transcribing room. She always liked to arrive before her students. Students in Division A were returning today—their first class after

Keeping the Record Straight

spending six weeks at Tri-City Hospital. Because the cooperative plan required that two students share one position at the hospital, Division B students would exchange places with the A group. Mrs. Lyndon would soon find out how well her students had performed on the job. She quickly selected tapes and cassettes in preparation for today's lesson. "How things have changed. . . ." She remembered when secretaries took dictation by shorthand directly from doctors. Now most medical transcription was done with mechanical equipment; hospitals used systems that utilized magnetic tapes, wires, disks or belts. Central dictation systems could bring information for transcription to a main information point. Telephone units enabled doctors to dictate reports, histories and progress notes as soon as they completed their examinations of patients.

Mrs. Lyndon was abruptly brought back to the present by the laughing, on-rushing sounds of boot-clad girls spilling into the room from the crowded corridor. "Hi! Mrs. Lyndon. Hello! Mrs. Lyndon. We're back! Mrs. Lyndon." The girls reluctantly settled down in their seats.

Mrs. Lyndon moved down a center aisle and sat on a vacant desk. "Now let's hear all about it!"

"Well . . . to start with, they use cassettes like we used in class," Velma said, opening the discussion. "As a beginner, I started with transcribing routine physical examinations of new employees. I was able to do eight

CAREERS IN THE HEALTH FIELD

a day. Then I was assigned to transcribing patients' physicals. A good transcriber types about 60 words a minute."

Doris spoke next. "I did x-ray reports, Mrs. Lyndon. At first, they were employees' x-rays; later I moved on to the clinic patients'."

"Tell me about the medical terminology. How did you find it?"

"Rough! Really rough! But we're getting used to the abbreviations now. Our unit supervisor gave us copies of medical dictionaries and reference books to help us with spelling and enunciation. The hardest was getting used to the foreign accents and drawls of some of the doctors. Some talked like cowboys!" Giggling and happy to be back together, the girls excitedly reported their experiences.

Mrs. Lyndon listened quietly for a while and then held up a box of tapes. "Today we will listen to several kinds of foreign accents; then we'll move on to drawls, nasal speech, slow talkers, fast talkers—all kinds of speech patterns you'll hear in your work as *Medical Transcribers.*"

Twenty students from Division B were assigned to a *Stenotyping* pool. They worked for various business offices in the hospital, such as accounts, admitting, payroll and purchasing. They learned to complete and process claim forms from the many insurance companies servicing the patients. They learned a great deal about Medicare application payment forms, pharmaceutical and dietary requisitions, disability claims and billing.

Keeping the Record Straight

At times, they were called to take dictation directly from a department head or a doctor.

"I was so scared," Karen reported to the girls at lunch. "He saw my hand shaking, so he offered me a cup of coffee. He said, 'Just relax—I'll go slowly so you can get it all down. I'll spell out the complicated words for you. Please don't be afraid to ask me to repeat something. I don't mind.'" Karen had survived with two minor errors, and Dr. Rao had congratulated her.

The girls kept their machines clean and remembered to disconnect them between typing assignments. Supplies were neatly stored in a large cabinet; the students took turns stocking and tidying the shelves. Above all, they learned that accuracy in their work was paramount, whether it concerned a decimal point or a misplaced comma.

Miss Rudell, coordinator of Aldrich's medical assistant program, had to recommend three girls as possible *Medical Secretaries*. They would work directly with senior medical secretaries in the offices of heads of departments. These students would need highly developed typing and transcribing skills. Their reading ability had to equal that of most college freshmen. In addition to secretarial skills, Miss Rudell's courses had stressed the need for a broad knowledge of medical terms, drugs and instruments, as well as acceptable initials and abbreviations for medical terminology. Her students understood and accepted the code of ethical conduct required of persons handling confidential data. Although the three would be assigned to different offices, their duties would be similar. Miss Rudell met with the hospital cooperative supervisor to define them.

"The girls will handle telephone calls and make appointments, in addition to taking dictation and transcribing correspondence and departmental matters," the supervisor said. "Occasionally they will be asked to check medical journals for items of interest to the departments. They may also assist with the proofreading of articles, lectures and manuscripts."

Miss Rudell thought for a moment, then replied: "Three of my best girls should work out—Maria for the surgical, Theresa in the chemistry laboratories and Mimi in pathology. We'll call them in and tell them."

The students were pleased, and promised to prove worthy of Miss Rudell's faith in them. Her parting instructions were: "Read the hospital manual! Check with your immediate supervisor to be sure you're following hospital policy at all times. Good luck, girls!"

Mr. Parker, Tri-City cooperative supervisor, checked the roster again. "I have about 15 more students to assign. Would your high-school course, Introduction to Programming, prepare a student for general entry-level work?"

The guidance counselor consulted the course description. "It certainly would; in fact, it includes on-the-job instruction. What did you have in mind?"

Keeping the Record Straight

"Well . . . the hospital has a very active computer center. Our people construct programs that handle data-processing jobs for accounting, engineering, dietary, pharmacology, purchasing and other hospital departments. Aldrich students can begin as trainees and earn full pay while they learn the fundamentals of programming through class work and in the computer center. They'll learn about computer systems and the mechanics of operation. Eventually, they will work with a variety of computer systems, as well as with different types of computer schedules and applications control."

Mr. Simon seemed puzzled. "That sounds rather sophisticated for high-school seniors. Could they manage it?"

"Oh, yes! We have learned that academic background is not the major factor. We look for alertness and an ability to concentrate on a specific problem, an analytic mind, an enthusiasm for challenge and ability to work with others."

Mr. Simon took the roster from Mr. Parker. "All right. Here are your trainee *Computer Programmers*—Miguel, Wayne and Louise."

Mr. Simon accompanied Mr. Parker to the main administrative office. "Are there students who would be interested in all-around office work?"

"Yes! Some students have a variety of secretarial skills of varying levels of proficiency. These students will probably advance themselves by on-the-job training rather

CAREERS IN THE HEALTH FIELD

than with higher education. They're employable now! They type, take dictation at about 100 words a minute, know simple bookkeeping and office procedures and can operate adding, duplicating, calculation and bookkeeping machines. These boys and girls fall into the category of *Typist/Clerk* or *General Clerical Personnel*."

Mr. Parker looked down at the roster. "We could use six typist/clerks in this office. Let's see if we can get volunteers."

Miss Henrietta Holt replaced the receiver and turned to her visitors, Mr. Simon and Mr. Parker. "A *Unit Clerk* spends a great deal of time on the telephone. I make calls to doctors, clinics, labs and pharmacology all day long! I relieve the nursing staff as much as possible from answering the telephones. . . . There it goes again. . . ."

"Faulkner Wing 8. Miss Holt speaking. . . . Yes, Room 12 is ready. . . . Would you please repeat that? . . . KRATER . . . T as in Tom? ARNOLD . . . diagnosis . . . hypertension . . . Dr. Gitlin's case. . . . Thank you!"

Miss Holt continued to make notes on a large pad. "Now I'll make up a chart for the new patient, put ice water in Room 12 and put his name on the bed and the door."

She was interrupted by a messenger whose cart held packages, assorted plants and fresh flowers. "Will you please sign for these, Miss Holt?" he asked extending a receipt pad.

Keeping the Record Straight

Miss Holt checked the names against her ward census sheet and signed. "These four are still here, but Miss Moore was discharged this morning. Please return this plant to the package room." A soft beeping sound caught her attention. Several lights were blinking on the Executone (desk monitor for intercom systems). She pressed one lighted button. "May I help you?" She released it to hear the patient's response through the intercom. "I'll tell the nurse right away." Miss Holt stepped to the closed door of the conference room and tapped on it as she opened it. "Excuse me—Mr. Harper in Room 14 is complaining of severe abdominal pains." She eased the door closed and picked up the receiver before sitting down. She quickly dialed the operator. "Please page Dr. Paskow, medical resident, for Faulkner Wing 8." She replaced the receiver with one hand and pressed another button. "May I help you? Yes. . . . The barber comes about 11:00 A.M. on weekdays. I'll put you down for a shave and haircut, Mr. Nolan." She wrote the information on a yellow barber request form. "All unit clerks record T.P.R.s [temperature, pulse, respiration] on the charts. I try to get them on early before the doctors make rounds." The telephone rang. "Faulkner Wing 8. Miss Holt speaking. . . . Yes. . . . Dr. Paskow —Mr. Harper in Room 14 is complaining of abdominal pains. I'll tell the charge nurse. Thank you." She dropped the receiver and leaped toward the closed conference room door. In her pink smock she bumped the door

CAREERS IN THE HEALTH FIELD

open wide, and in a staccato outburst she announced the emergency. "Dr. Paskow is on his way up—he wants to order two units of blood on standby, full abdominal prep, alert the surgical staff and get consent slip ready!" The conference room emptied as nurses and aides rushed to carry out the orders.

The telephones were quiet now, and Miss Holt was completing her weekly requisition forms for stationery, chart material, lab slips and desk supplies. A stack of lab reports were waiting to be attached to charts; she would do those next. Miss Holt gathered up the pile of library books left by patients discharged earlier; the volunteer would collect them tomorrow. The elevator door opened, and a messenger carrying a suitcase pushed a wheelchair through the opening. A gaunt-looking man wearing an overcoat two sizes too large sat slumped over in the chair. "Good afternoon, Mr. Krater. I'm Miss Holt, the unit clerk; I'll show you to your room." Miss Holt accepted the admission slips and addressograph or nameplate (similar to a charge plate) from the messenger; she then bent forward to make certain that those numbers on the plate were identical to the ones on Mr. Krater's wristband. Miss Holt led the patient and his wife to Room 12. "Please push this button when you want something," she said, demonstrating the intercom system. "Someone will answer from the desk through this speaker. Now get undressed and into bed. Mrs. Cunningham, the charge nurse, will be in soon to welcome you

Keeping the Record Straight

to our hospital." Miss Holt returned to the desk and stamped each sheet of Mr. Krater's chart with his nameplate. She picked up the telephone and dialed the operator for the final time that day. "Please page Dr. Carrera for Faulkner Wing 8; we have a new admission."

The last five students had been assigned; they would begin a two-week orientation and training program designed to give all new unit clerks an opportunity to become acquainted with the hospital, the personnel with whom they would work and the role of the unit clerk. Mr. Parker explained that 40 hours would be spent in the classroom and 27 hours in supervised practice in the nursing unit to which the clerk is assigned. This practice would be supervised by the charge nurse and the hospital's classroom instructor.

"Suppose we review some of the personal characteristics that are important for unit clerks." Mr. Simon was having Cokes with the three girls and two young men who were to be trained as unit clerks.

"Neatness, good handwriting, courtesy and good speech," volunteered a girl chewing on a candy bar.

"Don't talk with your mouth full," chided her friend. "How about being careful to get everything straight—messages, I mean. Work fast under pressure! Friendly and cheerful, because people are sick and worried. Smile! Check everything twice! Assume some responsibility, but know your limits! Dependable! Follow the rules! Well

CAREERS IN THE HEALTH FIELD

organized! Cool and calm! Plenty of patience! Get along with people!"

Mr. Simon threw up his hands as if to fend off the barrage of excited responses. "All right, all right—I think you'll all make great unit clerks," he said with a hearty laugh.

Pay day is a special day anywhere. But for Division B students, it was an occasion. Most of the students were seated near each other in the large cafeteria. Checks were being examined and compared.

"How much did you get, Wayne?"

"I'm a trainee, remember? I got $55. What about you?"

"A beginning typist/clerk gets $84 a week."

"Are you going to get that cute dress at the Tia Maria Boutique?"

"No, not this week. I'm saving for a pair of boots first."

"I'll keep half of my $115 until next week. Medical stenographers do better than transcribers—eh, Velma?"

Velma studied her check of $98 before answering. "Not bad, but I'll catch up. I'm saving mine for college. I'd like to get an A.A.S. degree in legal secretarial science."

Karen sat moodily staring at her check of $96, which represented a week's pay for a beginning stenotypist.

"What's wrong with her?" asked Miss Holt of one of the unit clerk trainees.

"She got more than my $50, but she borrowed so much there's not much left."

Eight ▶

THE FRONT DESK

Dr. Mel Kerns had completed the examination, but his patient, Charles McCall, was still lying on the examination table. "You may dress now; I'll send Mrs. Hairston in to help you. When you have finished, please return to the waiting room. I'll be with you shortly."

Dr. Kerns collected the chart and stack of x-rays and walked toward his office. He closed the door quietly and spoke to the back of a tall, regal-looking figure. "Mrs. Hairston, will you please assist Mr. McCall? He's finally agreed to surgery. Arrangements will have to be made at Tri-City Hospital." Mrs. Hairston turned and faced the doctor, nodded and headed for the examination room.

Mr. McCall was sitting on the edge of the table pulling on his shirt. Even this limited activity left him panting. "I'm so tired and weak lately. If an operation will relieve that, I'll gladly have it!" Mr. McCall sighed wearily.

"Have you made any plans, Mr. McCall? I mean about your job? Your family?"

Mrs. Hairston was buttoning his white shirt and adjusting the red tie. The brightness of his tie against the shirt seemed to deepen the pallor of Mr. McCall's haggard face. "You'll have to spend at least two to three weeks in the hospital and then about three weeks convalescing. Can your family manage?"

"Yes. I have some paid sick and vacation time that I can use, and I own a comprehensive insurance policy."

Mrs. Hairston looked up from the squatting position she had assumed to tie his shoelaces and smiled in relief. "With today's high costs for medical care, a person needs extensive coverage."

Stacey Hairston, R.N., had worked as a *Public Health Nurse*. In her visits to patients throughout the city, she had witnessed the devastation of family structure which often accompanied the hospitalization of the breadwinner. At times, families had to seek public assistance, move to cheaper quarters or even split up. Public health nursing appealed to Mrs. Hairston, because it afforded an opportunity to work closely with the entire family—not just the ill member. It also permitted a nurse to experiment with new ideas, to innovate and to see relationships between family and social problems. She learned a great deal about community health facilities and how to make the best use of their services. Mrs. Hairston had earned a bachelor's degree in nursing education and was well on her way toward a master's degree in public health nursing, with 25 credits in this specialty already com-

The Front Desk

pleted. After graduation, she planned to work as an administrator and teacher in a community mental-health clinic. Her sense of organizational responsibility, self-discipline, tact, flexibility and healthy outlook more than qualified her for such a career. Working with Dr. Kerns, a cardiologist (heart specialist), gave her the opportunity to study relationships between chronic illness and mental health. She understood the need for continuous supportive services to the ill senior citizen.

"Most people are frightened of hospitals, but they need not be if they are properly prepared. When you finish with Dr. Kerns, join me for a cup of tea and we'll talk about your coming hospitalization—something like a dress rehearsal." Mrs. Hairston guided the hobbling Mr. McCall to a large comfortable-looking chair near a window, and then continued on to the outer office.

If there is any one place that needs a skillful, attractive diplomat, it is the reception area of the physician's office. When a patient is greeted by a cheerful, gracious, smartly dressed receptionist, his aches and pains can seem less painful. Miss Angela Knox was *Medical Assistant* to Dr. Kerns. Her immaculate white uniform and shoes matched the professional look of Mrs. Hairston's attire. Angela did not wear a cap, but Mrs. Hairston wore a bit of shaped white, crisp organdy which identified Tri-City Hospital's School for Nurses. Angela completed a ten-month training course for medical assistants at a local

CAREERS IN THE HEALTH FIELD

technical school. The curriculum included survey courses in psychology, medical terminology, ethics, medical law and office procedures. She had learned typing, shorthand, transcription and simple bookkeeping while in high school. When Angela came to work for Dr. Kerns, the doctor and Mrs. Hairston taught her laboratory skills; Angela could draw blood samples and perform simple tests, take x-rays, electrocardiographs and blood pressure and give injections under their supervision. Her ability to respond quickly and quietly to emergency situations made her a valuable office team member.

Angela deftly juggled the telephone between her left shoulder and tilted head. The melodic, soft low tones of her voice were soothing. "I could give you an appointment for Friday at 2:00 P.M. if that's convenient for you, Mrs. Plimpton. Fine! Then we'll be expecting you. Good-bye!" Angela replaced the receiver and reached for the charts in Mrs. Hairston's arms. "Hi, Angela. I know it's a busy day, but Mr. McCall has just consented to have surgery. Will you make the arrangements at Tri-City please?"

"Of course. I have to call them for some laboratory reports this morning." Angela scanned her appointment pads. On Monday, Wednesday and Friday, Dr. Brewster, who shared the suite of offices with Dr. Kerns, came in to attend to his patients. In between greeting patients and making appointments, today Angela would assist Dr. Brewster with a gastric analysis (examination of stomach

The Front Desk

contents) and a spinal tap test. She had learned to assemble the appropriate equipment, properly position the patient and assist the doctor during the treatments. Tomorrow she had to review patients' accounts and begin the monthly billing. But right now, there were several prescriptions to be renewed for Dr. Kern's patients. She lifted the receiver and dialed Crescent Pharmacy.

The admitting office is often called the nerve center of the hospital, because of its scope and complexity. In addition to directing the flow of patients in and out of the hospital, the admitting office has daily transactions with practically every department in the hospital. Those departments which work most closely with the admitting registrars or clerks include nursing, laboratories, patient accounts, outpatient, medical records and surgery. In a large institution, the director of admitting may have a staff of 35 to 45, including an assistant director, area supervisors and admitting clerks.

The three main areas of most admitting departments are patient reservations, preadmissions and the service area office that actually processes patients' admissions to the hospital. The latter may be categorized as admissions to private, semiprivate, obstetrics, pediatrics, ward and neurological units. Another service that may come under the admitting office is central information, which gives the admitting clerk the control numbers that are necessary for patient admissions. This unit may also handle all information calls on patient location and status. Transportation, which brings patients to the floors, laboratories and x-ray departments, may also be under the jurisdiction of the admitting office.

"I'd like to hear more about your plan, Ron. Why don't we set up a luncheon appointment for next week?" Barry Reade, administrative assistant in charge of patient services, was reviewing some of the problem areas in admitting with Ron Flagg, *Director of Admitting Offices*. Mr. Flagg was promoted from assistant director four years ago. Since then he had developed and introduced several new systems into the department.

"I'll check my calendar. This idea has to do with instant computation of our daily census. I'm really excited about it!" The men shook hands, and Mr. Reade closed the door, permitting Mr. Flagg to continue with the census figures.

"The bed count is 1,762 as of five minutes ago," reported the *Assistant Director of Admitting*. "I've checked with the *Reservation Clerks,* and I have their figures too." At most hospitals, the medical board determines which cases have priority over others for admission purposes. Tri-City had three basic types of admissions—elective, emergency and relatively urgent. "Let's have the bad news," Mr. Flagg said, grimacing at the master census chart.

"There are 68 electives, ten emergency and 15 relatively urgent reservations!" the assistant read from her notebook.

"I have a new clerk for that area. Suppose I take him over and introduce him to the staff?"

Bill O'Hara had trouble keeping up with Mr. Flagg's long strides. Bill qualified for the position of *admitting clerk,* because he was a high-school graduate, typed 40 words a minute and had clerical skills. His work experience included such positions as bank teller, assistant insurance adjuster and insurance claims clerk. Like all beginning clerks in the department, Bill would be paid $114 a week.

Mr. Flagg talked as they made their way along the crowded corridors. "The reservation area of the admitting department takes reservations for patients being admitted to the hospital. The admissions of outpatients are based on anticipated discharges. A patient may be admitted to an incorrect floor because a vacancy exists there, but he must be transferred to the correct unit as soon as possible. Our reservation area houses a bedboard of all patients in the hospital which shows a patient's location, time of admission and other vital data. This board also indicates all available beds in the hospital, patients that must be transferred to their proper services and conflict in room accommodations."

Mr. Flagg held the door open to permit Bill to precede him into the elevator and then continued. "Your specific duties are to take reservations from physicians or their secretaries, check all available beds each day, call in patients for admission and transfer patients when a change in accommodation is requested." Mr. Flagg ushered Bill into a large office and introduced him to his future co-workers.

The *Chief Reservation Clerk,* Willis Packer, was processing a reservation for elective surgery in the semi-private pavillion. "Bill, would you like to see how the reservation slip is completed before it goes to the preadmitting office? This will be your first lesson." Bill indicated that he would and moved closer to Mr. Packer's desk.

Mr. Flagg walked briskly toward the ringing telephone in the preadmitting office. "Hello. Preadmitting office. Flagg speaking!" He listened, chuckled and replaced the receiver. "The bed count is 1,764; we just added twin girls," he said to the *Preadmitting Clerk,* who was busily sorting the admission questionnaires. These questionnaires were one of Mr. Flagg's innovations. The preadmitting clerk sent them to patients scheduled for admission in order to obtain vital statistics, insurance information and other data needed for admission. When the questionnaire is returned, the clerk types up an admission package and all insurance forms. If there is incomplete information, the clerk telephones the patient and obtains it. Identification bands and control cards are typed next. These packages are filed and given to the admitting offices on the day of patients' admissions.

The Front Desk

"How do you get this information when it is an emergency or relatively urgent admission?" Mr. Flagg wanted to know.

"Because there is no specific date for admission and the patient is called as soon as a bed is available, we can take all information from the patient or a family member by telephone. The admissions package is typed immediately and then sent to the area admitting office where the patient is expected," the clerk informed him.

The door opened abruptly, and a face peered into the room. "Is Mr. Flagg still here? Neil wants to see him."

Neil Shorter occupied a small cubicle at one end of the semiprivate admitting office, the largest of all area admitting offices. Neil's major responsibility was the making of addressograph plates. With the use of an addressograph machine, he cut plastic plates which showed the patient's name, sex, age, identification number and hospital location. These plates accompanied a newly admitted patient to the receiving floor. Neil was a graduate of a technical high school, where he completed courses in introductory techniques of printing. He learned how to set type, prepare makeup, lockup and feeding and carry out hand and power presswork. Neil also made and maintained an accurate master file of plates for names and addresses of all employees, department heads and visiting medical staff. He was frequently asked to run off mailing lists for bulk mailing. Because all Tri-City employees carried identification plates with photographs, Neil and his assistant operated a Polaroid-type camera for the pictures they affixed to the plates. These two clerks also performed miscellaneous duties, such as filing, stuffing and mailing envelopes, giving and receiving information by telephone and running errands.

"Glad you had a minute," Neil said to Mr. Flagg. "It's about a new kind of color film Jack and I have been trying out. I think it has sharper color tones, makes clearer pictures and is durable. We would like permission to order a carton."

Mr. Flagg studied the sample pictures. "They are definitely better. Go ahead. We'll stretch the budget somehow," he said jokingly.

The taxi entered the "Quiet Zone" and pulled up in front of Tri-City Hospital. A *Doorman,* dressed in a navy and gold-braided uniform and cap, stepped to the curb and opened the door; he escorted the passengers to the canopied steps. Mrs. McCall passed the overnight bag to the *Transporter,* who gently assisted Mr. McCall into a wheelchair. "Good afternoon! Which admitting office please?" asked the transporter as he expertly propelled the chair up the ramp. "Faulkner Semiprivate? We'll take the elevator at the end of the hall."

The crew of 20 transporters worked out of the transportation area of the central admitting office. Their duties were to safely transport new patients to assigned floors and other patients to various hospital departments

The Front Desk

for examination, tests and treatments. Frequently they assisted the *Messengers* in the emergency delivery of drugs, supplies and equipment. The transporters were basically a young group whose ages ranged from 18 to 26 years; the very nature of the work required one to be in excellent health, move rapidly, practice safety measures and demonstrate a genuine concern for patients' welfare. For these entry-level positions, no previous experience was required, and most transporters and messengers eventually advanced to positions requiring more skills.

Miss Pam Gould, the *Admitting Clerk* of Faulkner, was interviewing Mr. McCall. "Your policy provides for complete coverage in semiprivate accommodations. For the type of surgery planned, your hospitalization should last no more than three weeks. Dr. Kerns has also recommended convalescent care at Resthaven, the hospital's convalescent facility."

Miss Gould continued to talk as she assembled the papers on her desk. "Miss Knox, in Dr. Kerns's office, forwarded your x-rays, laboratory reports and admission summary as soon as we placed your reservation in the relatively urgent category."

Miss Gould removed the Ident-Band from the McCall Admission Package. "Please hold out your left arm, Mr. McCall. This bracelet identifies you to all of the staff." She snapped it securely; the circle could only be removed now by cutting through the plastic. "We have a small laboratory across the hall. The forms are ready for the blood tests. After you finish there, the transporter will take you to the x-ray department and then to Faulkner Wing 8."

Miss Gould reached across the desk for the telephone and dialed quickly. "Hello! This is Miss Gould in admitting. How are you Miss Holt? Mr. Charles McCall has just been admitted to Room 16—the A bed. Dr. Kerns has scheduled him for surgery day after tomorrow, and he will be transfered to I.C.U. (intensive care unit) immediately afterward." The clerk came around the desk to shake Mr. McCall's hand. "We hope your stay at Tri-City will be beneficial and as pleasant as possible under the circumstances." Mr. McCall thanked her and prepared to leave. The transporter picked up the suitcase and guided the wheelchair through the door.

"There are 12 of us here now, but more will come later," the spokesman for the group volunteered. These were fellow employees of Charles McCall; they had come to the blood bank to contribute the many pints of blood needed for Mr. McCall's heart surgery. Each donor completed a brief questionnaire designed to obtain medical history. The staff nurses recorded the temperature and blood pressure readings of the group. A medical resident was on duty to certify donor suitability and take care of emergencies if necessary. "I'm Cheryl Jarmón, an *I.V., or Intravenous, Nurse.* I draw blood samples for tests, introduce intravenous fluids and perform venous punc-

The Front Desk

ture for blood donations. Two donors will supply Mr. McCall with one transfusion of blood or plasma. After you have made your donation, return to the lounge please. There you can relax and enjoy some refreshments." The men and women were staring apprehensively at her. Miss Jarmón understood their anxiety. "Please try to relax. We'll take three people at a time, and the whole thing will be over before you know it. Are you the first volunteers?" Miss Jarmón jokingly asked three robust-looking young men making a hasty retreat to the rear of the room.

The transporter maneuvered the wheelchair and suitcase into the already crowded elevator. Mr. McCall's preadmission tests were finished, and he was on the way to Faulkner Wing 8. Dan, the *Elevator Operator,* ran the car from a half-sitting position on a tall stool.

Dan had been a taxicab driver before a serious accident led to the amputation of his left leg. After months of therapy and training, he could comfortably wear the prosthesis (artificial limb) for about ten hours a day. Dan was formerly self-employed, but with the combined loss of cab and limb, he had to seek a new career. His position as elevator operator provided an outlet for his jovial, garrulous personality; his wit often brought smiles to the sad, pain-creased faces of the passengers. Dan's salary didn't equal his former earnings, but he was happy in his new work. Tri-City employed male and female elevator operators to man freight, staff, patient and visitors' elevators. Some cars were manually operated, but others were of the self-service type. The operators assisted patients on stretchers and in wheelchairs in and out of the cars. Their duties also included transportation of freight in and out of the elevators. In an emergency call, they were expected to respond promptly and give whatever aid and assistance possible. The operators were generally on duty every day between the hours of 6:00 A.M. and 10:00 P.M.; after 10:00 P.M., all elevators were self-serviced.

"Good afternoon Mr. McCall. Your unit is ready," said Miss Holt in greeting the new patient. "After you have undressed and relaxed a bit, Mr. Reade, our *Administrative Assistant in Charge of Patient Services* will be in to see you."

Mr. Reade's main area of responsibility was making sure that a patient's hospital stay was as comfortable as possible. All complaints from patients and visitors were received by his office. To limit these to a small number, he tried to anticipate and care for the special needs of patients. These might include special visiting passes to visit the very young or very old patients whose working family members could not be free during scheduled visiting hours. Often it meant enlisting the doctors' cooperation and then granting permission to bring in familiar ethnic-type food. Sometimes patients felt more at ease in their own wheelchairs, under their own blankets and with their heads on their own nonallergic pillows. Mr.

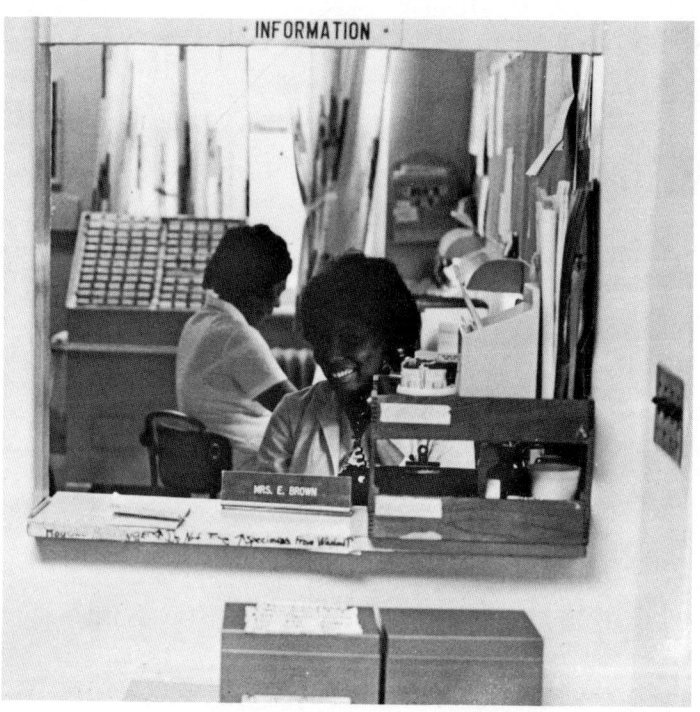

A **Unit Clerk** greets patients and visitors and performs clerical tasks.

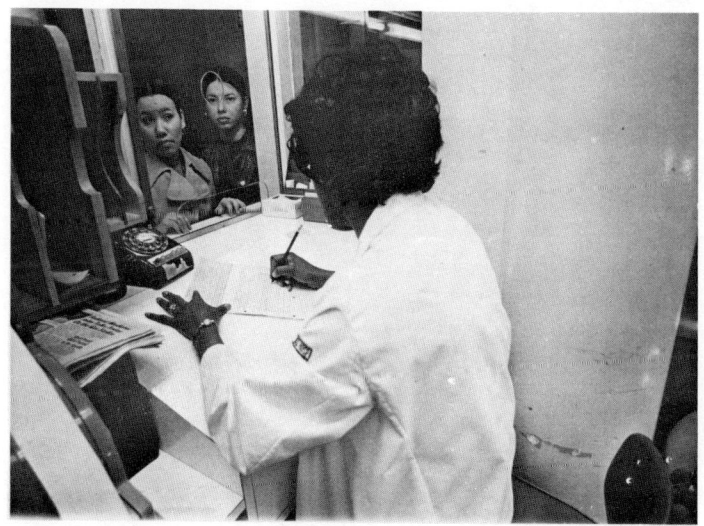

An **Admissions Clerk** completes one of the many forms which provide vital information about incoming patients.

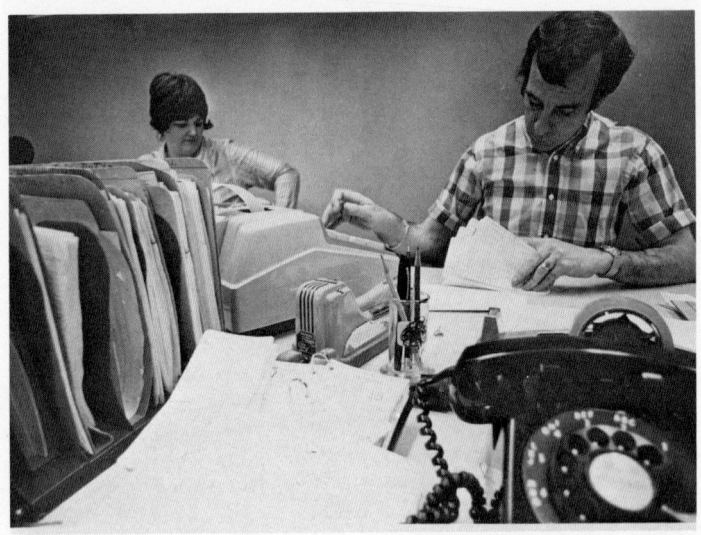

Hospital bills must be paid; Clerks and Billers tabulate and prepare patients' accounts for payment.

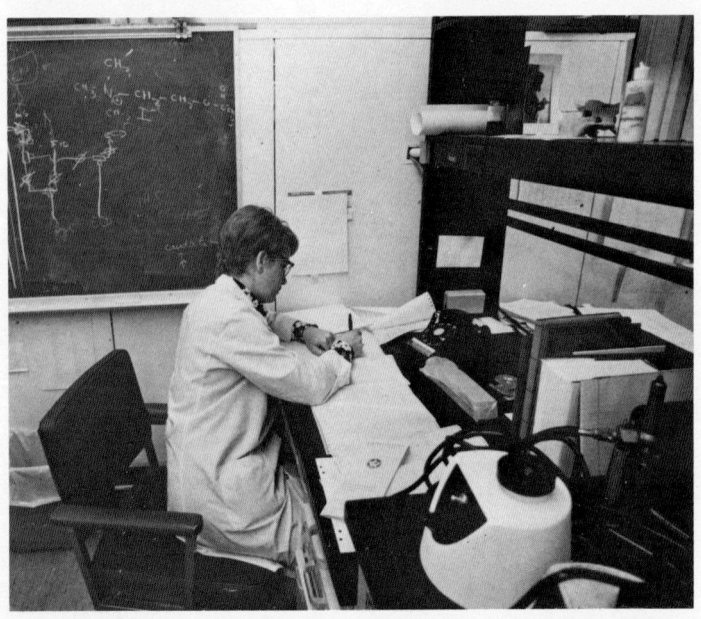

An Instructor prepares for the following day's lectures.

Attending lectures and seminars is an important part of all hospital on-the-job training programs.

The hospital library is available to professionals and paraprofessionals for study, research or relaxed reading.

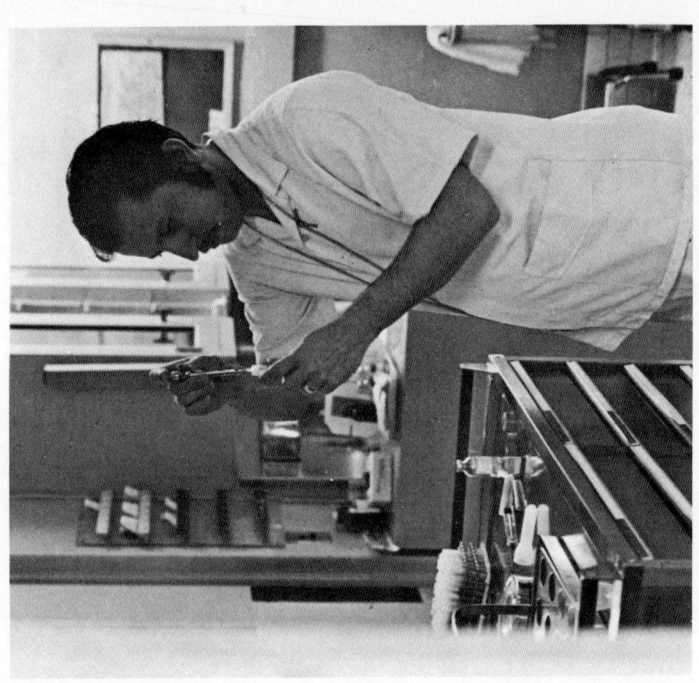

Performing tests on blood and other fluids is part of a Medical Laboratory Technician's responsibility.

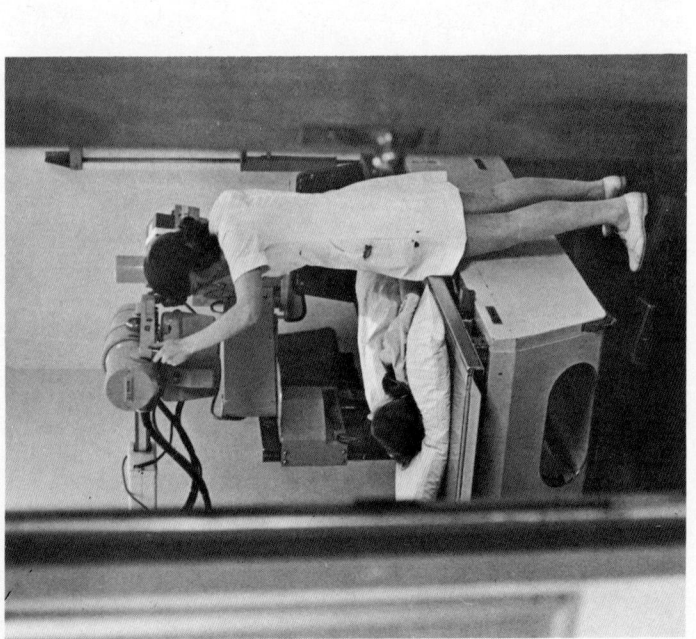

An X-ray Technologist carefully positions patient and equipment for a clear and accurate picture.

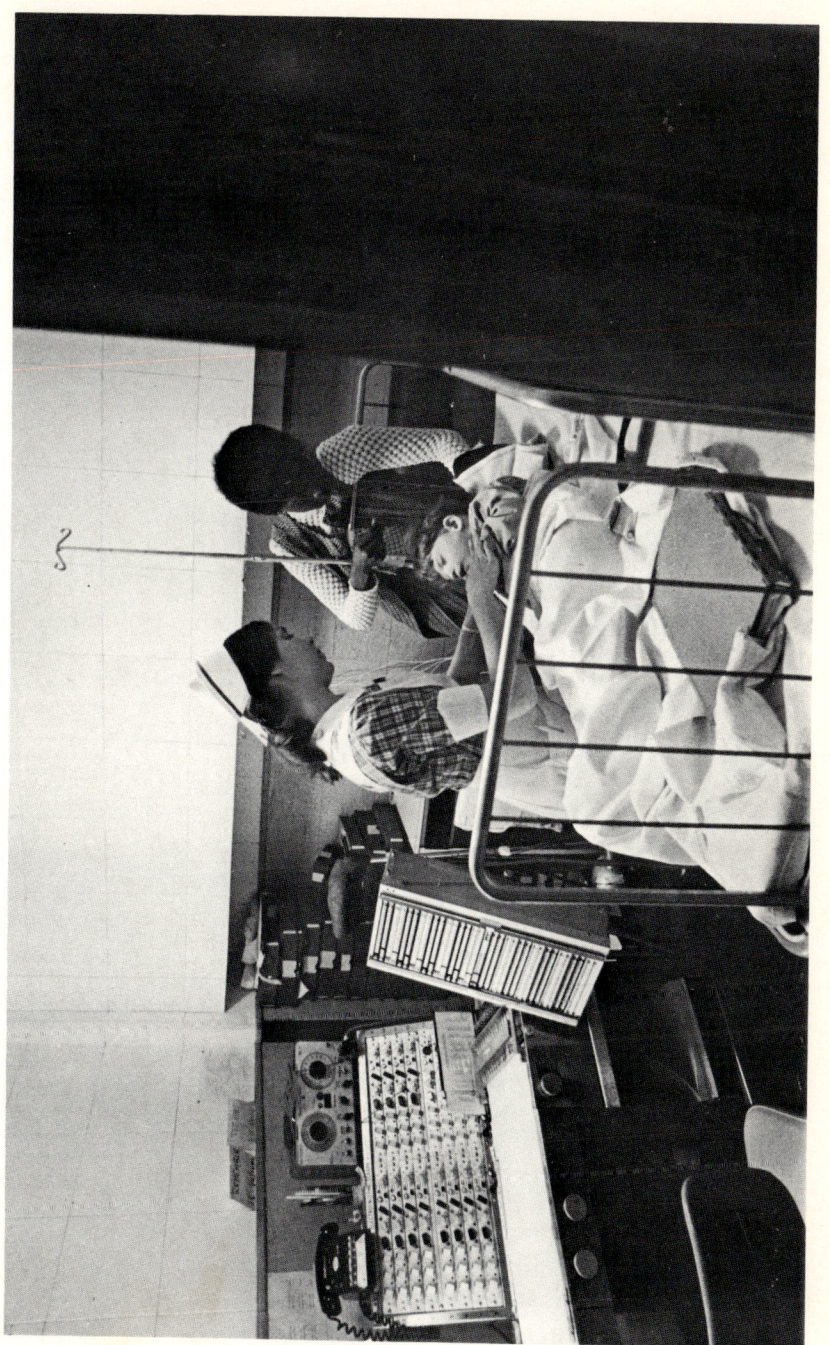

A Student Nurse comforts a young boy.

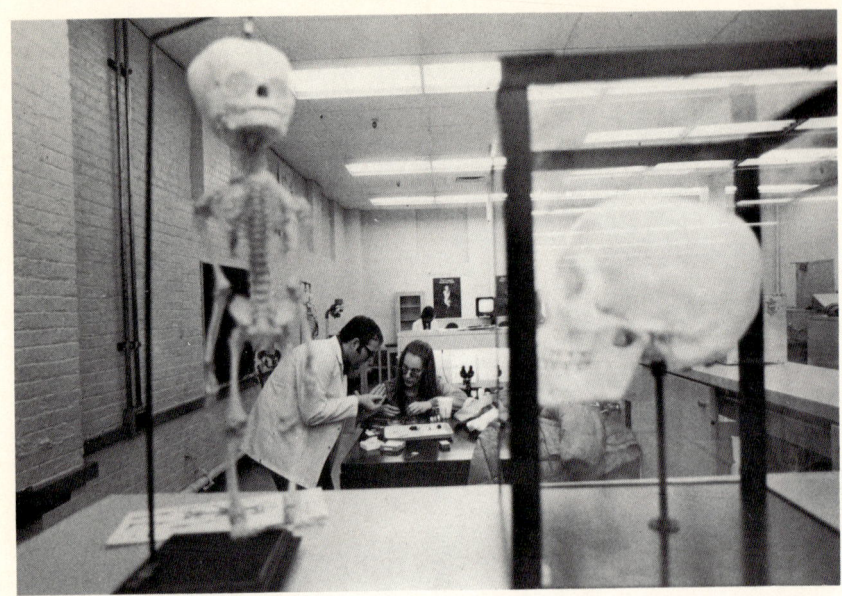

Students in an Anatomy laboratory work on projects of special interest.

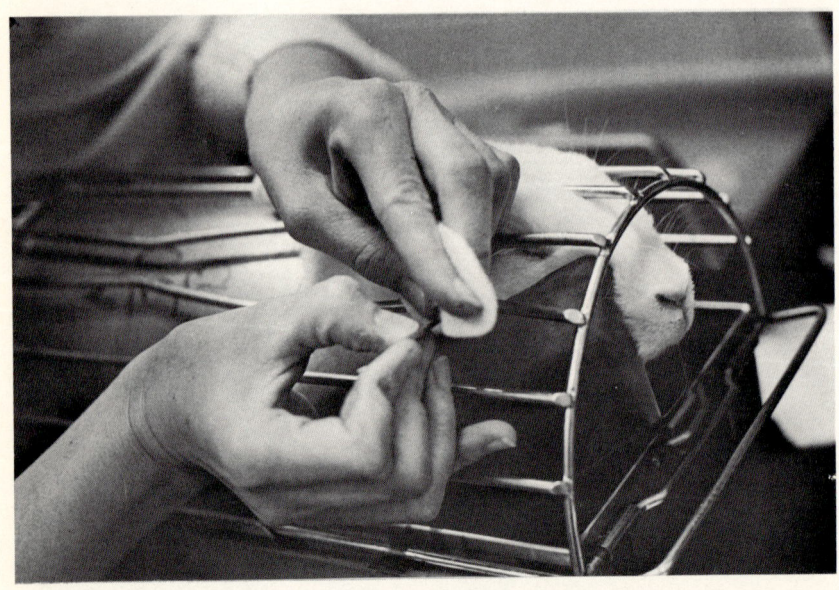

One of the main functions of a Pathology Assistant is assisting with important tests and research using small animals.

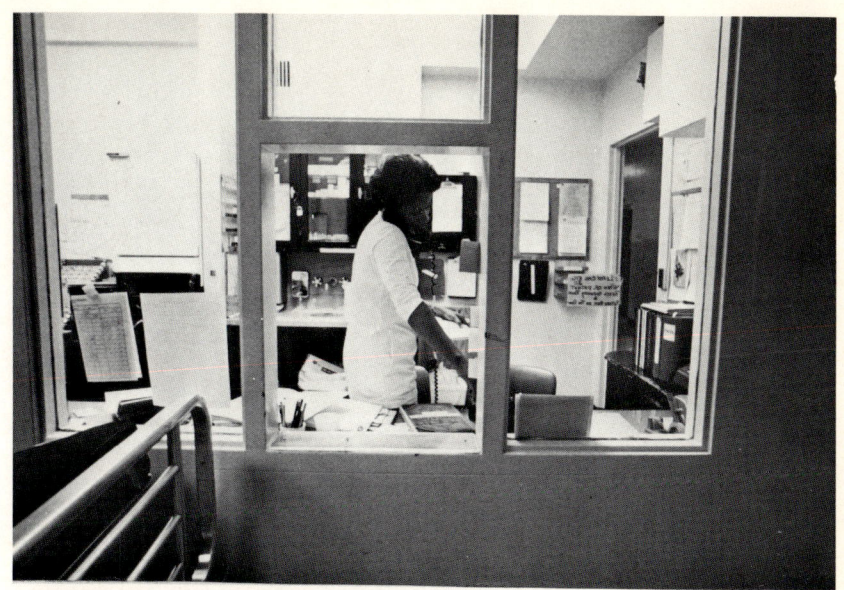

In order to coordinate patient care, a Charge Nurse must have frequent contact with all hospital departments. Below, a Charge Nurse gives a doctor a telephone report of a patient's condition.

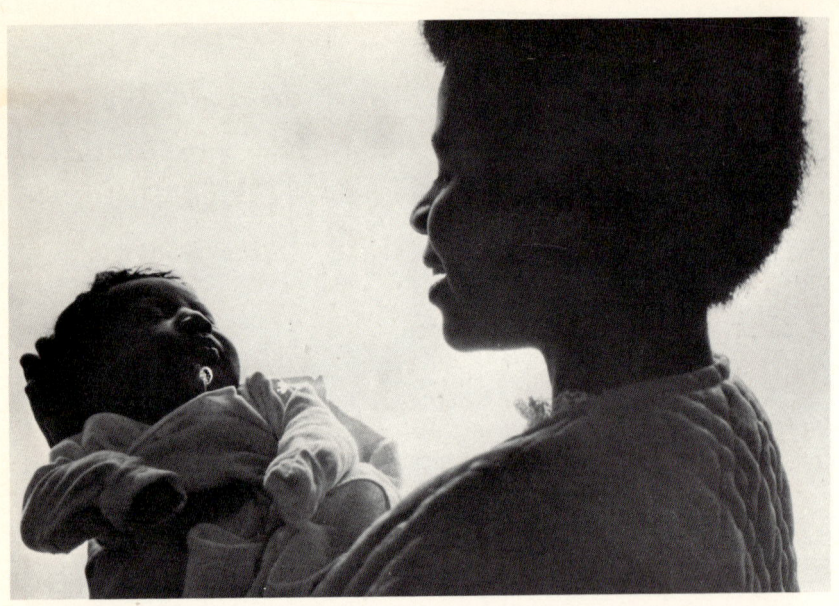

A Nursery Nurse brings a healthy first-born to his mother for feeding.

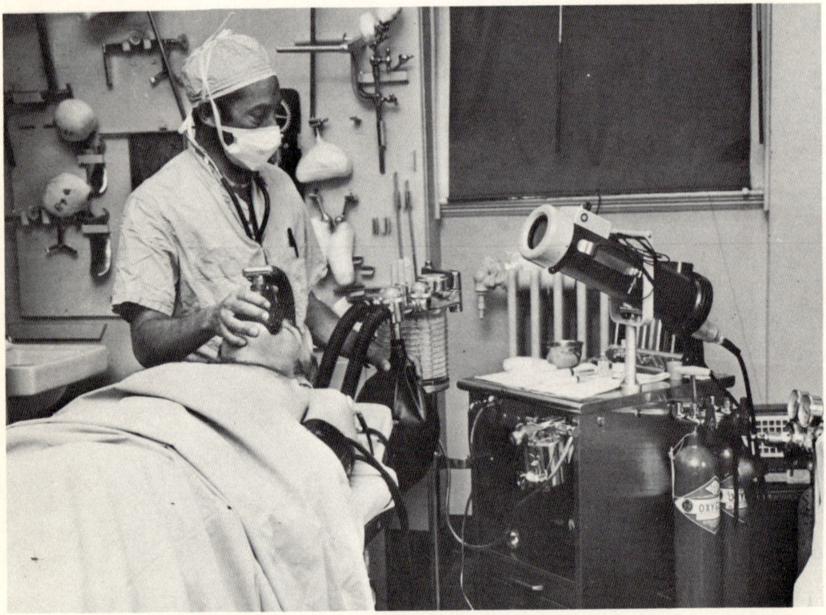

The Anesthesiologist is an important member of the surgical team.

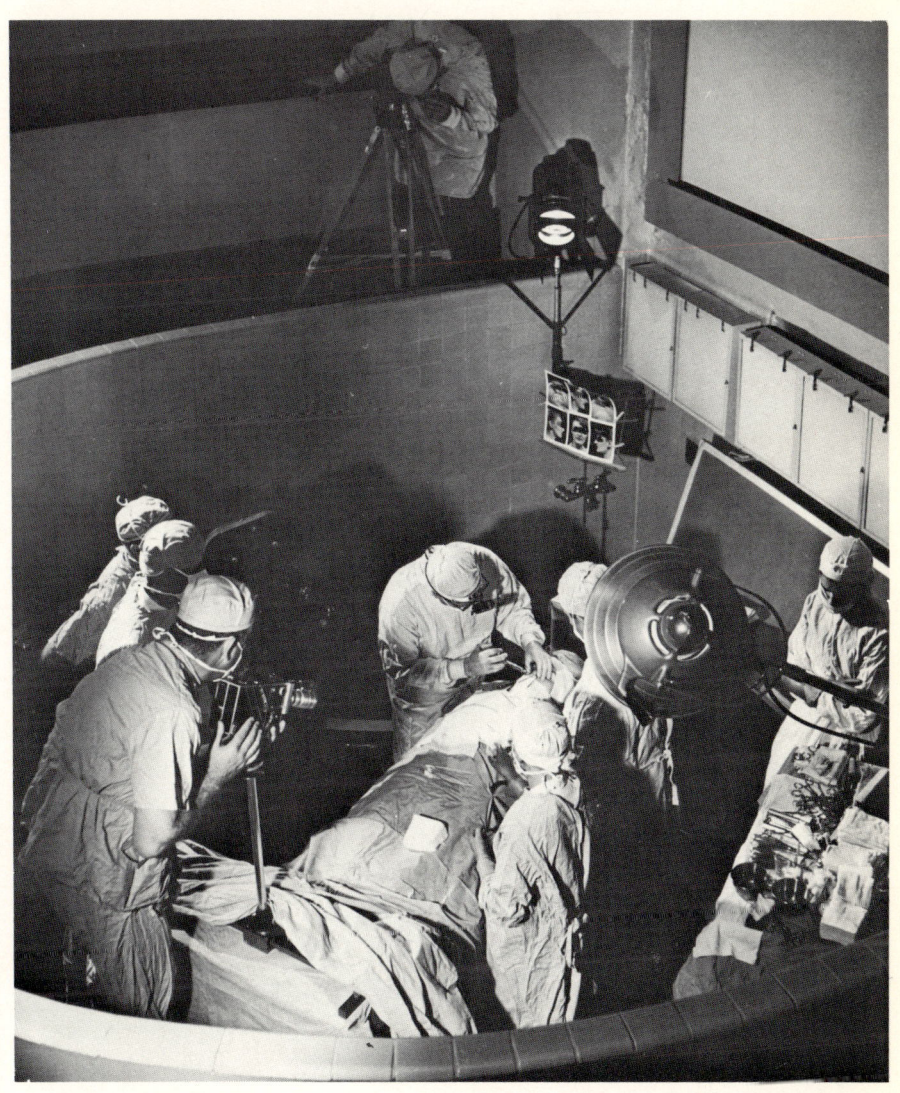

The Hospital Photographer often makes pictorial records of major operations.

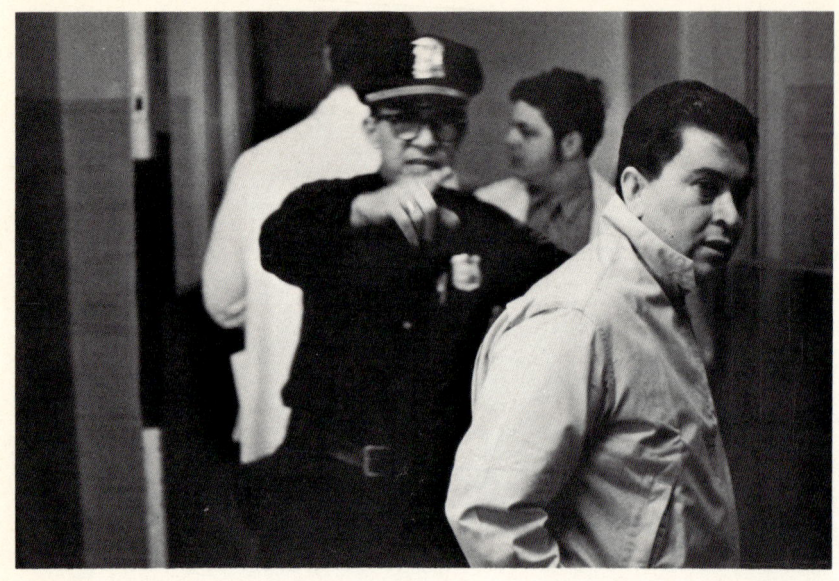

Security Guards also assist visitors with information and directions.

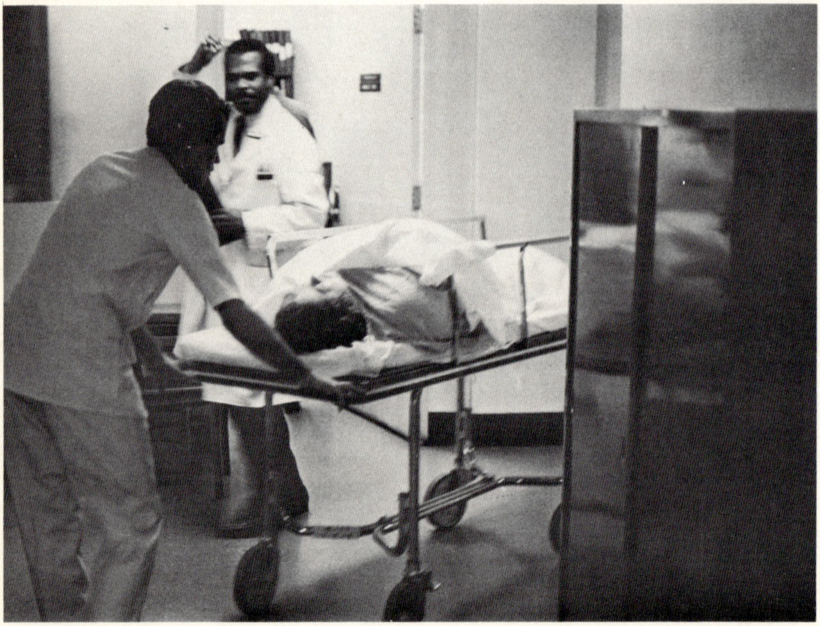

A Transporter is responsible for the safety and comfort of a patient in his care.

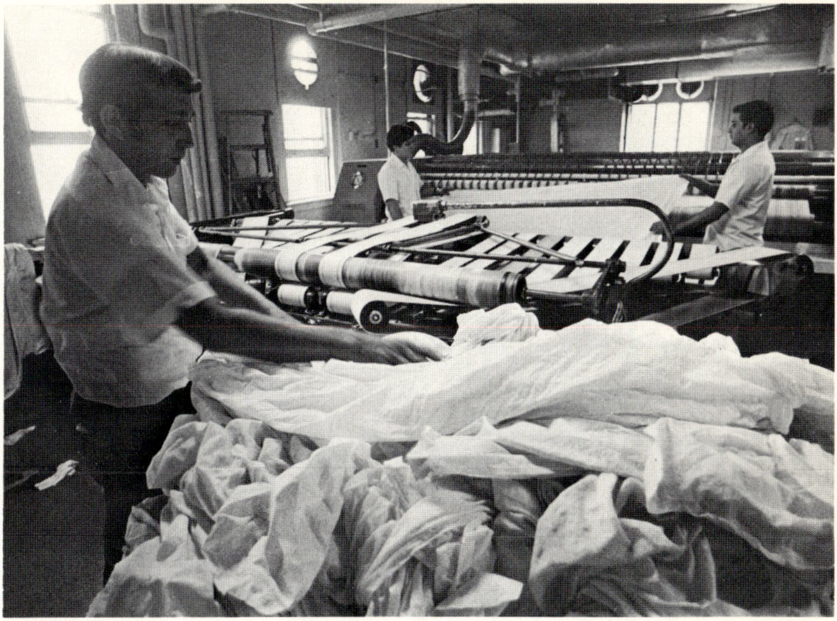

Not even a hotel uses as many sheets and towels as a hospital. Laundry workers use modern washers, extractors and driers.

General Cleaners, Porters and Floor Waxers keep hospital floors and walls sparkling clean.

Dietitians review patients' food selections to be certain they meet dietary needs.

Diet Aides select and place a variety of food on trays moving along a conveyor belt.

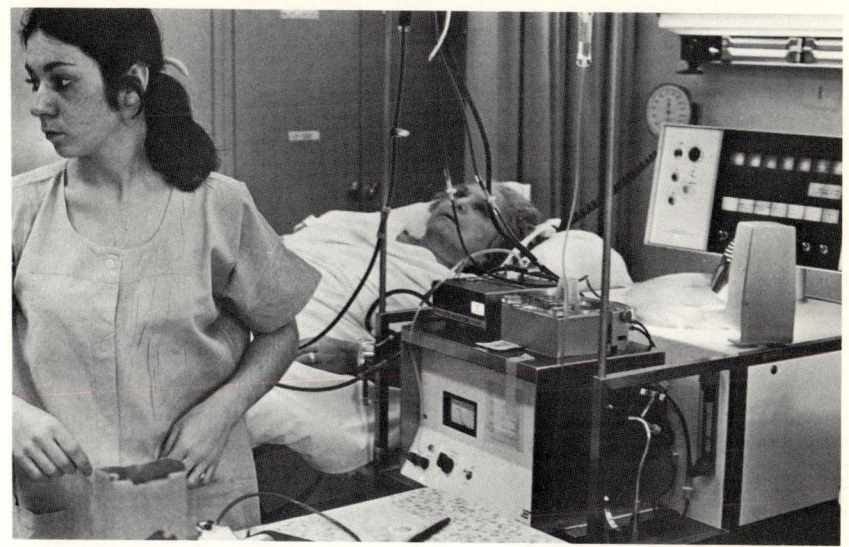

A Biomedical Equipment Assistant makes scheduled inspection tests on complex equipment in the Intensive Care Unit.

A Biomedical Equipment Repairman uses his on-the-job training to clean and repair a suction machine.

An Electrician checks the electrical supply system, which must fulfill the heavy demands of equipment, services and maintenance.

Skilled craftsmen design, construct and repair furniture in the Carpenter's Shop.

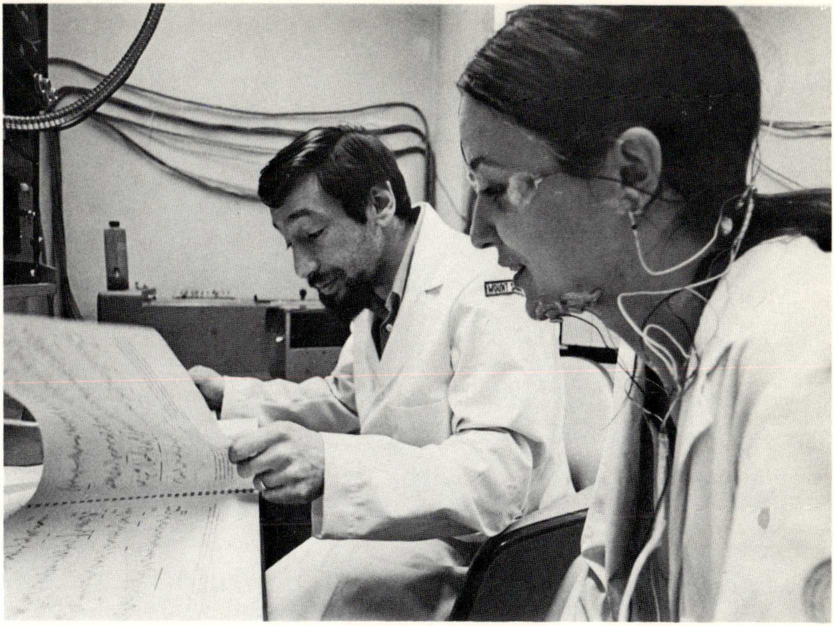

Two hospital staff members study recordings of normal brain waves taken by an Electroencephalograph Technician.

The Audiologist is one of many persons involved in the hospital rehabilitation programs.

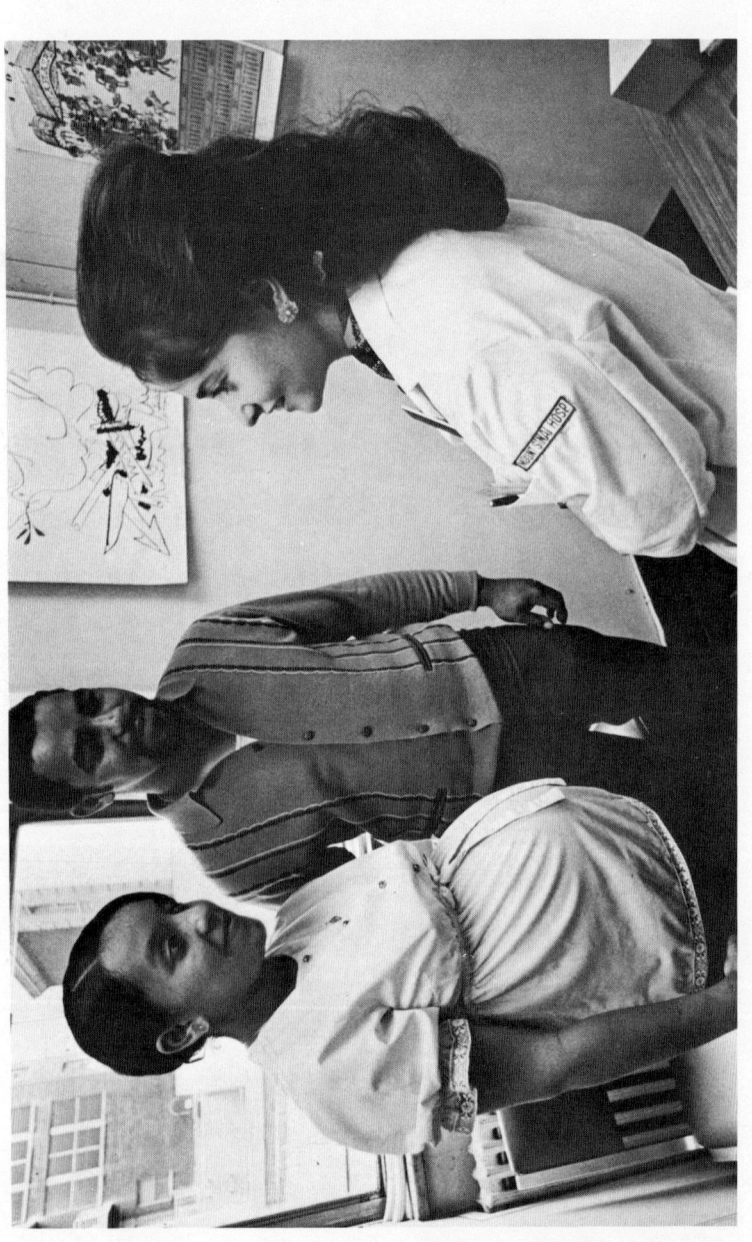

A Social Work Technician helps prospective parents plan for their baby's arrival.

All Photos Courtesy Mount Sinai Medical Center of New York City

The Front Desk

Reade was compassionate and sympathetic and allowed the patients these small comforts. At other times, a patient might need to be assigned to a special area on the floor, because of a hearing or visual problem. Mr. Reade's functions were designated by the director of public affairs, his immediate supervisor. Mr. Reade's present classification was entry-level for administrators. He was a recent community college graduate with a major in industrial and labor relations, although his interest and talents were in the field of journalism. It was in this specialty that he planned to earn a bachelor's degree. With experience, he hoped to move up within the department and work solely on publications, newsletters and management communications for internal and external use. His present assignment called for tact and patience in dealing with difficult patients and emotional relatives. Sound judgment, objectivity and empathy were other qualities possessed by Mr. Reade.

Mr. Reade sat facing Mr. McCall, who was in bed with his head propped up by three pillows. "Now let's review briefly how we have planned your stay with us." Mr. Reade cleared his throat and continued. "In preparation for the surgery, we have more than 15 pints of blood credited to your account. The reservation has been made for at least a three-day stay in I.C.U. (intensive care unit). When you return to this room, special nurses around the clock will be assigned to you. For this first week, visitors will be limited to your immediate family.

CAREERS IN THE HEALTH FIELD

Because Mrs. McCall is employed, I will issue a pass allowing her to visit before and after her working hours. A week before your anticipated discharge, Mr. Delacorte, a *Social Worker,* will arrange for your transfer to Resthaven.

He paused and looked up at Mr. McCall. "Thank you so much. I fought coming here for so long and worried so much about the operation. Everyone has been so kind and understanding. I'm almost looking forward to it now."

Mr. McCall forced a feeble smile in Mr. Reade's direction. "Here's my card. Please call if you need to. Be well soon!" Mr. Reade returned the chair to its place by the lamp table and quietly left the darkening room.

Nine ▶

SAFE AND SOUND

"But I know she was wearing it when we left the house. I saw it!" Mr. Gann's florid face wore a strained look, and his voice was slowly rising to a crescendo pitch. Mr. Reade gently maneuvered him onto a chair. "I'm sorry. I didn't mean to shout, but the ring is valuable! Please try to find it. The ring's been in her family for years! We're sentimental about it," pleaded Mr. Gann.

"Would you please describe it to me?" Mr. Reade asked in low, even tones.

"It's a pear-shaped diamond with several small emeralds in a platinum setting."

"I'm sure we'll find it. Why don't you let me handle it?" Mr. Reade asked Miss Holt to put through a call to security. She did and passed him the receiver. "Hello! Phil? Could you come up to Faulkner Wing 8? It concerns a lost ring. Thanks!" Mr. Reade sighed in relief and returned the receiver to Miss Holt.

Phil Lyman was *Chief of Security* for Tri-City Hospital. His staff of 30 guards patrolled the buildings, gardens and streets bordering the hospital. Mr. Lyman was a retired city policeman who held the rank of captain before his retirement. He personally selected his staff of *Security Guards*. Some were former bank guards, railway policemen or members of private security forces; others were recently discharged veterans with military police experience. All carried sidearms, clubs and walkie-talkies, and their blue-gray, military-type uniforms were visible at all hospital entrances, parking lots and exits and in the network of subterreanean corridors.

Day and night the guards patrolled the buildings, punched time clocks and maintained an alert for the unusual—including fires, theft, floods and malfunctioning of heating, plumbing and electrical systems. The guards investigated lost or stolen property and received found property. Occasionally the security men had to enforce hospital policies regarding misconduct, such as smoking in restricted areas, profanity, gambling and fighting. At times violent or disturbed persons had to be subdued or controlled; when necessary, the guards could solicit the aid of local police. In addition to vigilance, Mr. Lyman looked for self-restraint, composure, agility, gentleness and ability to handle controversy when selecting his force.

"Mr. Gann, I'd like for you to meet our security chief, Phil Lyman. He will try to locate your property." Chief Lyman folded his six-foot-plus frame and lowered it to

Safe and Sound

the edge of the black and white tweed-covered club settee facing the still agitated Mr. Gann. "Please give me the details as you remember them," the big man requested in a soft gentle voice. Mr. Reade had to hurry to the private pavilion if he was to keep his 11:00 o'clock appointment with the chief of maintenance. His watch warned him that he had five minutes left. He glanced toward the two men engrossed in animated conversation; they didn't even look up as he quietly shut the door.

For the past two months, the Shaaker or private pavilion had been undergoing a colossal redecorating project, floor by floor. Mr. Flagg, director of admitting, blocked admission to certain rooms so that whole sections of floors could be available to the various crews involved in the renovation. The odor of paint reached Mr. Reade as the elevator stopped at the 12th floor. He could hear the hammers and saws of the carpenters. There were 25 rooms on this floor, and each was scheduled for refurbishing. The decorators had selected colors, furnishings and accessories; now Alfred Bagley, *Chief of Maintenance and Engineering,* was supervising the men who would carry out the colorful themes.

Mr. Bagley was with a *Plumber* and a plumber's helper in room 1202.

"Have I kept you waiting, Al?" Mr. Reade wanted to know.

"No! We're a bit behind schedule today. We have some new men."

CAREERS IN THE HEALTH FIELD

Mr. Reade caught a glimpse of three young men in new green coveralls attentively watching the plumber install pipes for a new shower. "Exactly what does a *Plumber's Helper* do?" questioned Mr. Reade.

"Oh! Many things. He assists the plumber in laying out, assembling, removing and installing pipes, fittings and fixtures, pipe-fitting and cleaning drain lines. He keeps the plumber equipped with materials, tools and supplies and cleans work areas, tools, equipment and machines. A helper performs routine plumbing procedures, such as cleaning drains and removing blockages, too. Look over there—they're cutting and threading pipes."

Mr. Bagley's brow wrinkled in a puzzled frown. "You're not think of becoming one, are you?"

"No, just interested. It's their noise that's disturbing some patients on the 11th floor."

"There's something wrong with that yellow. It's just not right!" The *Painter Foreman* was directing his criticism to the crew of six painters.

"It needs some white; it's too gold," volunteered one of the painters.

The rooms and baths were to be painted in pastel shades of yellow, blue, green and turquoise with white trim. The six *Painters* were participating in the apprenticeship program sponsored by a local labor organization; their training period lasted three years and included

Safe and Sound

work experience and related classroom instruction covering a minimum of 144 hours each year. On the job, apprentices learned the care and use of tools such as brushes and spray guns and how to match and mix colors and erect scaffolds. In the classroom, they were taught color harmony, paint chemistry, how to estimate costs and the techniques of mixing and matching paints with wall papers. All were high-school graduates, and three had experience as house painters. Each had successfully passed an aptitude test and medical examination. As first-year men, their wages were $3.25 an hour—half of the hourly rate earned by journeymen (skilled craftsmen).

"Suppose each of you try to mix a sample that matches the color chart," the foreman suggested. "I'm due at the regular joint committee meeting." The foreman left, and the painters hastened to complete their assignment.

The monthly meetings were held to evaluate the kinds of skills learned by the apprentices, to plan for continuing on-the-job experiences and to develop job categories in accordance with the goals of the hospital, unions and labor group.

Mr. Bagley called the meeting to order. Seated at the round table were David Welpin, personnel director; Stuart Greenidge, head of building services; Edwin Lawton, vice-president of O.S.E. (Opportunities for Skilled Employment), a local community group; Michael Bonomo, director of Apprenticeship Programs for the

CAREERS IN THE HEALTH FIELD

Building and Construction Trades Council; and various hospital employees.

"The program is coming along well and Tri-City is ready to enlarge apprenticeship opportunities. Mr. Greenidge can tell us of job categories, union or otherwise, that need to be developed," said Mr. Bagley. Stuart Greenidge's small-framed body disguised a dynamic and authoritative personality. Throughout the hospital, the Head of Building Services had earned a reputation for getting the job done. He donned his horn-rimmed glasses, cleared his throat and spoke in a deep, resonant voice.

"The hospital is continuously expanding and renovating, but at the same time maintenance and services must be kept at top-level performance. I could use *Refrigeration Mechanics, Electrician's Helpers, Carpenters, Air-Conditioning Installation and Maintenance Men, Furniture Repair and Refinishers, Tile Workers* and *Tile Setters, Plasterers* and *Utilities Mechanics*." Stu Greenidge put aside his notes and continued. "Mr. Welpin has some new categories which require no experience, only an ability to follow simple directions and a willingness to begin at entry-level work. Want to report on these, Dave?"

Mr. Welpin stood up and distributed some papers to those present. "These are job descriptions of our latest offerings." The group read that a *Light Man* was responsible for replacing light bulbs throughout the hospital.

Safe and Sound

His immediate supervisor was the electrician foreman. The light man occasionally repaired or replaced switches, fuses, sockets and other lighting components. He could also wash and replace glass and plastic light shades; keeping the work cart stocked, the electrical shop neat and tidy and transporting supplies were also his duties.

"You notice that to qualify for the job of *Metal Cleaner and Polisher,* a man only needs to be healthy, agile and willing to work in and out-of-doors. He cleans, removes minor rust spots and polishes and maintains such metal surfaces as stainless-steel entrance doors, window frames, canopies and flag poles," Mr. Welpin explained. The sheet also described a *Shade and Drapery* man as one who removes window shades and blinds. He measures windows for new shades or blinds, takes down the draperies, tags them for cleaning and rehangs the clean draperies. He follows a four-to-six-month cycle in covering all areas of the hospital.

The group continued to read the sheets, but Mr. Lawton spoke up to say: "Here are two positions that should be attractive to our young men who are vocational high school graduates. The *Office Machine Serviceman* needs mechanical aptitude, manual dexterity and competence in simple arithmetic. A *Television Service and Repairman* requires mechanical and analytical aptitude, finger dexterity, good vision and color perception and the strength to lift 50 pounds."

CAREERS IN THE HEALTH FIELD

"I suppose these jobs average $2.10 an hour?" Mr. Lawton asked of Dave Welpin.

"Yes—and there are three others that don't require any diplomas. Take a look at the *Furniture Mover, Floor Buffer* and *Touch-Up Painter* jobs. As entry-level positions, these five are perfect for young people who need time to develop definite vocational skills and commitments. They can gain work experience while maturing and investigating career possibilities."

Mr. Bagley turned to Mr. Bonomo. "How do the unions feel about the program?"

"They're quite satisfied. There are now over 75 apprentices in 14 different specific trades assigned to Tri-City Hospital. Our goal was to open up opportunities for people wanting careers in the health and hospital industries, and we're doing it!" he said with conviction.

"Suppose we hear the other reports during lunch," Mr. Bagley proposed. "Mrs. Young, our administrative dietitian, has prepared a delectable repast for us as usual." The conference room door swung open, and two diet aides pushing a serving table ahead of them entered the room. The table held delicious-looking salads, tea sandwiches, fresh-fruit cocktail, petit fours and beverages.

Mr. Bagley was sorting the requisitions prepared by various foremen in maintenance and building services. Milton Teasdale, the *Chief Purchasing Agent,* spread several attractive folders on the table. "These products are being used in many western institutions and with reported success. They cost less because it's a promotional deal and can be utilized all over the hospital."

Mr. Bagley read the literature on soaps, powders, cleansers and antiseptics. "We'll give them a try. But will I get my air conditioners and floor waxers this month if I cut a few corners?"

As chief purchasing agent, Mr. Teasdale bought the supplies necessary for the efficient functioning of all departments of the hospital. Because he bought everything from computers to bedpans, Mr. Teasdale was knowledgeable about many products. Since an efficient purchasing agent's responsibilities go beyond buying, he understood the broad program and goals of Tri-City. Mr. Teasdale exercised good judgment in making decisions affecting the functioning of his department as it contributed to these goals.

Al Bagley and Milt Teasdale had been classmates at State Technical Institute. While Mr. Bagley majored in mechanical technology, Mr. Teasdale concentrated on accounting and business administration. After graduation, Milt worked as one of the assistants to the chief purchasing agent. During the first two years, he became acquainted with the many hospital procedures and thousands of different items used in the operation of a hospital. Milt's understanding of basic business procedures fostered a sensitivity to the market's best buys, enabling him to stretch the constantly limited funds available. His open and informal manner made it easy for him to get along with people. "I think your *Locksmiths* are pleased with the new locks. One sent me a note of thanks. It's my first fan mail!" Mr. Teasdale said proudly.

The responsibilities of the *Chief of Maintenance and Engineering* are great, since the comfort and safety of both patients and staff depend upon the proper functioning of the hospital's plant and its equipment. The size of his staff may range from four to more than 100 workers, depending upon the size of the institution. As chief, Mr. Bagley supervised a large staff of highly skilled and semiskilled workers. His knowledge of plant operation and experience made him a valuable resource person and adviser to hospital administrative personnel. Mr. Bagley's sound judgment and managerial skills earned him a salary of $19,500 a year.

A hospital may provide efficient security services, a clean environment and essential mechanical, electric and electronic equipment, but to be completely "safe and sound," it must have a highly organized central service or sterile supply department. This department's personnel are responsible for the storage and distribution of the medical and surgical supplies and equipment related to patient care. Sarah Anderson, *Director of Central Supplies,* was giving a demonstration to new employees on how to operate the autoclave (a machine for sterilizing). "Be

Safe and Sound

sure not to overload and check the amount of pressure against the format on the chart," she said, pointing to a large plastic instruction sheet above the machine. "After the instruments are cleaned, they are wrapped into neat packages. Gloria will show you how to wrap and label them."

Gloria Asti worked as a *Central Supply Technician;* she cleaned and sterilized instruments and equipment according to a prescribed procedure and technique, using antiseptics or the autoclave as sterilizing agents. When in doubt, Gloria could refer to her instruction manual, which clearly described the contents of each kind of instrument set or package to be prepared. The sets were used in the operating rooms, clinics, treatment centers and patient units throughout the hospital. So that the instruments would always be in perfect working condition, Gloria and the other technicians honed, polished and repaired them periodically. The male and female technicians' ages ranged from 18 to 50 years; because most of the work could be performed from a sitting position, two of the staff members were physically handicapped. Skill in handling small instruments, manual dexterity and the ability to follow simple routines were the basic requirements for their position. The ability to read English at the ninth-grade level was important too. These technicians assembled and processed sterile and nonsterile treatment and procedure trays or packs, including surgical dressing sets. Many of the treatment packs that were once assembled and sterilized by the department now came in sterile, sealed plastic packages from sterile supply or hospital supply companies. These included intravenous and transfusion sets, stomach and urinary tubes, syringes and needles, used only once and then discarded.

Ronald Thompson was a *Central Supply Assistant*. Twice a day, he stocked his four-tier supply truck and made rounds to all of the floors in the Faulkner Building. On each floor near the nurses' station was a large sterile supply closet. Its shelves were clearly labeled for everyone to be able to quickly locate dressings, sets, packs, bandages and instruments needed in the care of the patients.

"Good morning, Ronald," Miss Holt called to the tall, slim man backing the truck out of the elevator.

"Hi, Henrietta! I got your message about the chest drainage packs, and I'll leave the four extras every day for as long as you need them." Miss Holt accepted the four cartons of disposable, plastic cups used by the nurses for measuring and distributing patients' medications. Ronald looked at his master chart, which showed the average amount of supplies needed for each floor based on the size and bed accommodation of each unit. He selected various-shaped packages from his truck and replenished the shelves. Because he was thorough and well organized in carrying out his duties, Ronald took time

Safe and Sound

to rearrange, sort and stack the supplies in a neat and orderly fashion. Ronald was a high-school graduate with no prior hospital experience, but Mrs. Anderson was impressed by the reports of initiative, ambition, reliability, flexibility and congeniality in the references he submitted. Mrs. Anderson found the references presented a true picture of Ronald's personality, and she planned to make him *Supervisor of Central Supply Assistants* after two years of service. This position paid $10,250 a year, which was about twice the amount of his present salary. As supervisor, he would assist her with the on-the-job training program; this four-month program was required of all new employees in the department. In addition to working experience, the new employees received formal instruction on such topics as medical terminology, packaging instructions and principles of steam and gas autoclaving, problems of cross-infection, ethics and safety and elements of work simplification.

Mr. Reade glanced at his watch; it was almost 7:30 P.M., and he had missed dinner again for the second time this week. He thought half aloud to himself: "Whatever made me think that an administrator led an easy life? More money equals more responsibility!" The ringing of the telephone jarred him out of the reverie. He grabbed the receiver. "Reade here! Oh—hi, Phil! You still working too? The missing ring?" He lis-

CAREERS IN THE HEALTH FIELD

tened for a few minutes and then exclaimed, "Wonderful! Wonderful! I'll file it under 'Happy Endings'! Good night, Phil."

He sat back and reflected on the irony of the closed case. Amid all of the excitement that accompanied Mrs. Gann's emergency hospitalization, Mr. Gann had neglected to lock his apartment door. He spent several hours at the hospital getting Mrs. Gann admitted and filing triplicate reports on the missing ring. When Mr. Gann returned home, he discovered that burglars had been active in his absence and money, jewelry and other valuables were taken. However, Mrs. Gann's ring was quite safe. Just before the stretcher was rolled into the ambulance, Mrs. Gann had passed the ring to her sister for safekeeping!

Ten ▶

COMMUNICATIONS

Mimi Devereau was practically skipping down the hall. Less than four months ago, Miss Rudell had assigned her to work as a medical secretary in the pathology department. At first, the work had been complicated and demanding, but Mimi worked hard to keep up. Then a very strange thing happened. The more she learned, the more she wanted to learn! Mimi didn't quite understand it, but one day, it became quite clear to her that her goal was to become a bacteriologist. Dr. Oreskes, chief of the department, explained the work and opportunities available to this kind of scientist. He even helped her select the most appropriate college. And today the acceptance letter arrived with a promise of a substantial scholarship! Mimi sang louder as she neared the door of the printing shop.

The several machines in operation were so noisy that Daren didn't hear Mimi enter. Daren Donohue was a *Printing Assistant.* His job was to perform routine printing and layout work using a variety of printing machinery and equipment. He could operate or use varitype, multilith, mimeograph, offset, paper cutting and Xerox. His immediate supervisor was the printer, whom he assisted with layouts and paste-ups. Tri-City issued several monthly publications, in addition to the many newsletters originating from various departments. Daren was busy at the collating machine. *Tri-City Voice* had to be ready for distribution today. Mimi pulled at the hem of Daren's purple coverall to get his attention.

"I have some great news, but I'll save it for lunch," she said in an exaggerated businesslike voice. "Dr. Oreskes would like 60 copies of this monograph, 'The Role of Pathology in Preventive Medicine.' Could you do them today?"

"Not today! But, for you—the first thing in the morning!" Daren took the copy and counted the pages. "See you in three hours, ten minutes and five seconds," Daren called to the back of Mimi's printed dress slipping out of the half-closed door.

"If we are to retain our September deadline, we will have to work much faster." Sam Rovner was dictating a memo to Frederick Marechal, *Chief Hospital Administrator* for Tri-City. "I suggest an early meeting of all those involved in the Annual Fund Drive."

Sam Rovner, *Public Relations Officer,* was an important member of the management team, and every year

Communications

led Tri-City's public appeal for financial help. "Are the news releases ready? Fine! Please get them to all of the newspapers today, including the local foreign language press! What about the public announcement spots for radio and television? Has Beth finished them?"

Beth Fergus, *Executive Secretary* to Mr. Rovner, was used to working under such pressure. She had started in the department as a stenotypist more than six years ago. Her ability to concentrate on and complete assignments ahead of schedule attracted Mr. Rovner's attention. When his former secretary took a permanent maternity leave, Mrs. Fergus replaced her. The public relations officer depended upon her to supervise the work of the seven clerical workers in the department. She assisted Mr. Rovner in promotional activities, such as "Hospital Careers Day" for high-school students and "Open House" for community residents. She completed three years of college, with a major in English, before marrying and withdrawing from school to join her husband overseas. Because of Mrs. Fergus' skill in language arts, Mr. Rovner relied upon her to edit leaflets, brochures and feature stories he prepared about the hospital. Mrs. Fergus kept an up-to-date resource file, from which she extracted human interest stories for the speeches Mr. Rovner gave to dozens of social and fraternal organizations during the year.

Mr. Rovner was an English literature major and had served for two years as editor of his college newspaper.

CAREERS IN THE HEALTH FIELD

After graduation, he worked as backup announcer for a local radio station for two years. Unfortunately for him, the announcers enjoyed excellent health. He joined Tri-City as *Assistant to the Public Relations Officer,* and three years later was promoted to his present position with a salary of $19,500 a year.

"Beth!" called Mr. Rovner over the interoffice telephone, "please check on the photographer. The pictures for our recruitment brochure should be ready."

Mrs. Fergus made a note on her pad under the heading "Things That Should Have Been Done Yesterday." She spoke into the telephone, "Consider it done."

Mimi pressed forward in the elevator and was the first one out when the doors clanged open. She was hurrying to meet Daren in the Coffee Shoppe. "Suppose he won't want to wait?" she thought. They had worked it out so carefully. She would work until Daren graduated from college; he had a year of work to complete toward a bachelor's degree in computer science. Now she had a chance to go to college too! But it meant postponing the wedding for at least another year.

"Mimi—over here," Daren shouted above the clatter of dishes. He was sitting with Guy Kimmel, the hospital's *Photographer.* "Look at these shots! You're in two of them, Mimi." Mimi picked up the photographs and started to sit down.

"I'm leaving. I hear Mr. Rovner's looking for his pic-

Communications

tures. See you two later!" Guy returned the pictures to the folder, pushed back his tray and made room for Mimi to squeeze into the cozy booth.

Guy worked part-time at Tri-City. When not at the hospital, he could be found in his father's studio across town. Guy's professional training included on-the-job experience, coupled with formal classes at the School of Visual Arts. He took photographs for purposes of publicity, fund raising, teaching and recruitment. Editors of the several hospital newsletters, alumni associations and employee-union publications made use of his services. In addition, Guy took pictures of retirement, award and promotion, anniversary and dedication dinners. His files were overflowing with mementos of happy times at employees' birthday parties, sports events, dances and boat trips. Because of his irregular schedule, Guy was paid an hourly rate of $10. He shared an office with Ivan Major, the hospital *Projectionist;* there was a small darkroom in the rear where Guy often developed black and white or color film.

"Hold on, Mr. Rovner—he's coming in now." Ivan handed the telephone to Guy.

"Yes, sir. I have most of the pictures ready. Could you get permission for shots of the new hyperbaric chamber? It's ideal for the fund drive publicity!" Guy suggested enthusiastically.

Ivan stored away the screen and slide projector; this morning he had shown slides of the architect's drawings and plans of the hospital's ten-year building program to members of Tri-City's board of directors. He consulted tomorrow's schedule. "Guy, would you please take down film No. 12, *Open Heart Surgery;* Mrs. Beacham's surgical nursing class needs it for 10:00 A.M. Dr. Whipple wants those film strips on cell structure for his hematology lecture at 11:30 A.M." Guy handed Ivan the film.

"Does it have to be rewound?"

"No! You know I always store my films properly!" Ivan said, feigning a sulky glare.

Ivan worked out of the public relations department; he reported there every morning to pick up conference announcements. With these and other requests, Ivan scheduled the time, location and type of film or slides to be shown the following day. He also obtained pertinent materials and equipment and set them up at conference sites. Often he rearranged the room for better viewing. Ivan learned how align the slides in a specified order and coordinate their advance without instructions from the narrators. After a showing, he rewound and spliced faulty film, boxed the slides or film strips and returned them to the neatly kept cabinets. Ivan had no formal training for his job, but had been trained by one of Mr. Rovner's assistants. He enjoyed the work, but three nights a week he joined Guy at the studio to study the essentials of good photography.

"Turn Mrs. Chase's face a little more to the right.

Communications

Good! That's a great shot!" Mrs. Chase, a life-size plastic female model, had been placed inside the hyperbaric chamber (a capsule-shaped tank of excessive atmospheric pressure). Leslie McBain, the *Hyperbaric Operator,* was posing at the monitors in a gleaming white and blue space suit. "Les—make believe you're turning the dial with your left hand," Guy directed.

Leslie was a new breed of technician; his position was created when Tri-City received this new lifesaving machine. A member of the medical team, Les sterilized, set up and maintained instruments and equipment used in chamber procedures. During a procedure, he recorded ECG (electrocardiograph) and blood pressure readings. Les also acted as backup chamber operator, assisting the doctors and nurses while another technician monitored the controls. He was ever on the alert for any irregularities in the apparatus. Les had been selected for the on-the-job training because he was intelligent, self-assured and reliable and could exercise good judgment. He quickly learned all the practical and formal details of operating the machinery. Les worked well with other members of the staff and volunteered to transport patients, collect a needed medication, stock supplies or clean up if necessary as his part of the team effort. Guy's camera continued to click away as he shot pictures from a high step-ladder, a table or bended knee or even spread out on the floor.

CAREERS IN THE HEALTH FIELD

"Thanks, Les—these will be just great in color," Guy commented happily. Looking up at the tall young man, he asked. "By the way—how's Tri-City's basketball team doing?"

"We're working on a 14-and-two record: we'll be All-City Champs again for sure!" Les boasted good-naturedly.

Harrison Forde, M.D., and Sam Rovner relaxed in the relatively quiet doctors' lounge. The view of the city from the 20th floor was particularly striking at dusk. The two men settled back against the plump, yellow cushions and put their feet up on two black vinyl hassocks. The fading sun cast long shadows across the floor, and an early springlike breeze gently stirred the sheer yellow- and green-striped curtains. Dr. Forde was discussing the research project which had become the most important thing in his young life.

"I think the public will take an interest in the project and understand its importance. If we can show the long-range effects of diet in infancy and early childhood on adult accomplishment, every American might have a chance to develop to his full potential!"

"You may have something there. You'll need the full cooperation of the medical records department, because my assistant will want copy within two weeks. Can you manage that?"

Dr. Forde swung both feet to the floor and jumped

up in one swift movement. "I'm halfway there!" he called over his shoulder as he passed out the swinging doors.

A well-organized medical records department is inherent to the smooth functioning of any hospital. The medical records of all former in- and outpatients are stored in a systemized way for easy retrieval. Mr. Robert Haber was *Chief Medical Record Librarian* and supervised other *Medical Record Librarians, Medical Record Technicians* and clerical workers. Mr. Haber and his staff planned, prepared and maintained records and reports on patients' illnesses and treatments. These professionals were prepared to assist the medical staff in research projects, develop auxiliary records, compile and tabulate statistics and develop systems for storing and retrieving medical information.

Mr. Haber had trained as a medical record technician at a two-year college. Upon graduation, he passed the professional examination given by the American Association of Medical Record Librarians and became an A.R.T. (registered technician). His first position with an insurance company lasted five years; because he lacked a four-year degree, his chance for advancement was limited.

Mr. Haber decided to return to college. He discovered that his previous education and professional experience were accepted toward the bachelor degree requirements. His formal classwork at college included courses in medical terminology, medical record science, administration

CAREERS IN THE HEALTH FIELD

of a medical records department and legal aspects and principles of the administration of health care agencies and institutions. The program prepared him for an administrative and supervisory position, which he found as assistant to the head of the medical records department at Tri-City. Three years later, Mr. Haber was chosen to direct the department of 20 librarians, technicians and clerical personnel; his salary advanced from $10,500 to $13,500 a year with the promotion.

"I can only spend a half-hour with you today. I teach a seminar in medical records science twice a week at a community college—my alma mater, in fact. Nancy will help you. She's quick and enjoys assisting young doctors with research. I'll call her."

Nancy Shumacher had worked as a medical record librarian for the health department in her home town before joining the staff at Tri-City. She was accurate, particular about detail and persistent in carrying out a task to completion. "I'll show you what we have to do, Dr. Forde." Nancy smiled and pulled over a book the size of a telephone directory.

Nancy leafed through the large classification book; she found the section and ran her finger down the page. "This is the code number for the type of anemia involved in your research. It's No. 240. Now we go to the five-by-eight index file and pull out all the cards under that code listing," Nancy explained, hurrying across the

Communications

room. "There should be quite a few; we started our research because of the unusual large number of cases. You're right. It looks as if we have more than six drawers of No. 240!" Nancy observed with a slight groan.

"What's on the cards?" asked Dr. Forde.

"We list the patient's identification number, sex and age, his doctor's name, dates of admission and discharge, race, type of surgery, treatment or condition and the results," Nancy answered. "I'll assign two technicians to the job. They'll make a list of the cases and then retrieve the actual charts from our storage area for you. With some clerical help, they can complete the job in about two full days."

"I'm amazed. What makes a good medical record librarian anyway?" Dr. Forde asked with growing interest.

"Well—accuracy under pressure and frequent interruption, arithmetical skill and a well-developed sense of professional ethics are important assets," Nancy summed up with pride.

Mr. Welpin was interviewing Miss Shirley Harley for the position of *Switchboard Operator*. "Tell me about your exprcrience," Dave Welpin urged. "Where have you worked?"

Miss Harley nervously pulled on the straps of her red shoulder bag. "I was with the telephone company for more than a year. Then I worked at a local bank for two more years. I can work several types of boards now."

"We use a multiple-position switchboard," the personnel director informed her, "so that's important. We plan to install centrex eventually. But, for the present, you will receive and route incoming calls and handle conference lines. There will be times when you will act as *Page Operator* and page hospital staff over various intercommunications systems, such as the loudspeaker or pocket short-wave radio." Mr. Welpin paused to give Miss Harley time to absorb the range of activities.

"I can handle all of that. I once worked for an answering service, where I was required to take and relay messages, place long-distance calls, send telegrams and record outgoing and incoming toll charges. I can also operate receiving and sending telegraph machines," Miss Harley finished with a slightly confident grin.

Mr. Welpin stopped writing and looked up. "It's important that you be able to relay calls promptly—but to the right person or correct department! So please read this booklet carefully to familiarize yourself with the general organization of Tri-City."

Mr. Welpin escorted Miss Harley to the outer office, where she would complete the personnel forms. He reread Miss Harley's references, then took his pen to underline such words as "alert," "clear diction," "patient," "informed," "extensive vocabulary" and "sound judgment."

Communications

"I must remind the operators to say, 'Good morning—Tri-City Fund Drive—don't forget to Give,' when they take incoming calls," he said to himself.

"It's true that first impressions are important and lasting. That's why we select our *Receptionists* with care." Mr. Welpin was visiting with the public relations officer. "Miss Sylvia Coleman is at the desk in Faulkner. Take a walk with me, and observe her in action."

The attractive Miss Coleman sat at a large desk in the main lobby of the Faulkner building. The white card on the desk read RECEPTIONIST in large black letters, but most visitors came to her for directions and information. Miss Coleman greeted each visitor as if she had been waiting just for him. Her large blue-black eyes were as friendly as her wide, easy smile. "Good afternoon. Welcome to Tri-City. What can I do to help you?" She came from behind the desk to greet the middle-aged couple. "Let me see the name, please," Miss Coleman requested, taking the slip of paper from the gentleman. "You're in the right building. Take the first elevator to the fourth floor, please." She walked them halfway across the lobby. A short man half-dragging a small boy hurried to Miss Coleman's side. "Please. . . . Miss! Miss! Where is obstetrics? I've got to get to my wife! Where can I leave Kerry?"

"I'll take care of him—obstetrics admissions is the office to your left. Good luck, sir. Come with me Kerry,

CAREERS IN THE HEALTH FIELD

we're going to the Play Pen." Sylvia Coleman reached down for the tiny wet hand.

The Play Pen was one of the projects of Tri-City *Volunteer Association*. These men and women of all ages operated the Gift Shoppe and the Traveling Library. Their bright orange smocks were frequently seen on the patients' floors and in the clinics. They shopped, wrote letters, made telephone calls and served evening refreshments to patients. Hospital rules prevented children under 14 years of age from visiting patients, so they were left in the care of a volunteer in the Play Pen. Toys, books, games, dolls and puzzles were purchased with proceeds of the volunteers' annual bazaar. Miss Coleman led the reluctant Kerry into the huge room decorated with circus motif. Simulated laughing clowns, elephants, tigers and monkeys were everywhere. In one corner, four children were aboard the whirling carousel. Six tots sat in a circle of small chairs, completely captured by the antics of a teen-age storyteller; cookies and milk lay abandoned on the round table. "I've brought a new friend—Kerry Oliver," Miss Coleman said to the volunteer in charge. Kerry accepted the big lollipop and darted for the red scooter. "I don't think he'll give you any trouble," Miss Coleman said as she left the Play Pen.

"Are all of your receptionists as attractive as Miss Coleman?" Sam Rovner asked.

"We have mature women and young men in these positions too," Mr. Welpin replied. "We judge an applicant on personal grooming, over-all appearance, outgoing and friendly personalities, speaking voices and general knowledge of the hospital. In a sense, you might say they're playing a big role in your field, public relations."

Eleven ▶

AUXILIARY SERVICES

Chandler Ferguson stood outside the gleaming glass doors and made a final check of his elongated reflection. The blue shirt had been a wise choice—not too flashy. Black shoes looked better than sneakers with the gray plaid slacks. His mother had been right as usual! This was a big assignment—a chance to interview a department chief. Chandler was a cub reporter for the *Bugle,* the weekly voice of Aldrich High School. A forthcoming issue was to be built around hospital careers that are not connected directly with patient care. Chandler's assignment was to write a feature story on Victor Bradford's department of patient accounts. Chandler ran the comb through his curly hair for the fifth time, pulled down the navy cardigan and sidestepped through the partially open heavy doors. His classmate Steve Bowman, *Bugle* photographer, had promised to meet him in the lobby. Chandler spotted the back of Steve's red varsity sweater. He was talking with a pretty receptionist.

Auxiliary Services

"Hope you don't mind the boys coming today, Vic," Sam Rovner said. "We encourage this kind of cooperation between the hospital and the high school. Your department has four separate units and employs six kinds of special skills; that should make an informative article."

Mr. Bradford, *Director of Patient Accounts,* continued to clear his desk of unanswered memos and mail. "I've prepared some materials for them to take back to Mr. Simon, the senior guidance counselor. Everyone's agreed to pose for pictures too!"

"Patient accounts has two major functions," Vic Bradford explained to Chandler and Steve. "The department bills patients and/or third-party payers. It also collects all money for patient services." Chandler was taking notes in his own style of shorthand. Steve sat on the desk loading the 35-mm. camera for the second time. "Our work falls into four areas—inpatient billing, outpatient billing, credit and collection and cashier services." Mr. Bradford continued to talk as he opened the office door. "The main office is partitioned into four units, each with its own supervisor. Come with me and I'll give you the grand tour," he offered.

The group followed Mr. Bradford to the section facing the tall windows. "In this section, our *Billers* prepare bills for patients or insurance companies for collection or refund overpayments." He motioned toward a short, obese woman seated behind a desk. "Kay Orrington supervises a staff of 20 in our inpatient billing."

CAREERS IN THE HEALTH FIELD

Chandler looked around the unit. "Is the work very complicated?"

"No. They double-check all charges for accuracy and prepare the bills," Mr. Bradford answered. "Sometimes our billers in the outpatient billing run into difficulties, because the patient is transient or in the excitement of the emergency gives incorrect information."

Steve got permission to snap pictures of a young man preparing a typical bill. "What is the starting salary for a person without experience?"

"About $5,200 if he's just completing high school and $5,400 and up with some experience," Mr. Bradford replied.

The credit and collection section was alive with ringing telephones and clattering typewriters. Jason Court, the supervisor, was conferring with two *Account Representatives*. They made room for the boys in the small office. Chandler scanned his prepared list of questions.

"What personal qualifications are needed for positions in this section?"

"A great deal of patience, an understanding of people and persistence!"

Steve looked surprised. "Don't people pay hospital bills?"

"Oh, yes, eventually—but very slowly and sometimes painfully! At times, the account representatives have to wait out court judgments, lawsuits, uncooperative heirs and estate claims before an account can be closed. This

Auxiliary Services

can take several years! So we require our staff to have a year of experience in collecting for hospitals, loan companies or private collection agencies before we hire them."

"Now over there our *City Investigators* work long hours trying to 'sue the city.'" Laughing at his own joke, Mr. Bradford pointed toward a far corner. "Kevin Goren, the supervisor, has just settled a case. Perhaps he'll tell you about it." Steve's camera recorded their winding progress through the large, cluttered room. Chandler continued making notes while the group moved in the direction of the glass-enclosed unit.

"All of my people are trained on-the-job. Formal education beyond high school is not required, but they must learn a lot and be quick! They must use common sense, sympathize with patients' problems but be objective. When a patient is unable to pay his bills and is not covered by any insurance plan, we try to seek reimbursement from a city, county or state agency." Mr. Goren paused. "For example, John Doe spent more than six months at Tri-City. He has no funds, insurance or resources. However, he is a minor and his surgery was part of a rehabilitative treatment plan. Because of these two factors, he is eligible for assistance from state funds issued out of H.E.W. (Department of Health, Education and Welfare)."

Chandler scribbled faster as Mr. Goren closed the patient's file, but he asked: "Does the patient have to apply?"

CAREERS IN THE HEALTH FIELD

"Not really. We interview the patients, contact the proper agency and process the papers. We try to remember that this is often embarrassing to patients and make the whole procedure as pain-free as possible," Mr. Goren explained.

"What are they doing?" Chandler asked Mr. Bradford. Two young women were seated before a long counter covered with IBM graph sheets.

"They control and evaluate all data for input to the computers. When necessary, they also check and correct all output from the computers. They are called *Control Clerks*. An aptitude for working with figures and typing skills are required for their positions."

Mr. and Mrs. Arnold Krater stood in front of the *Cashier*'s window. George Malicone studied the many entries on the bill. "You were with us for three weeks. How was your stay?"

"Very pleasant under the circumstances. Everyone was wonderful to me!"

Mr. Malicone checked the totals on his calculator again. "As soon as I enter today's charges, we'll have the final totals. Would you like a copy first? Make yourself comfortable in the lounge," he said, extending the papers to the former patient.

Mr. Bradford, Steven and Chandler watched closely from the adjacent lounge. "The cashier has to be very observant and make sure the charges make sense! For instance, suppose Mr. Krater was charged for obstetrical

Auxiliary Services

services!" Mr. Bradford speculated in a horror-stricken voice.

Mr. Krater wrote out a check and extended it to the cashier, who read it carefully. "Thank you! Here's your copy, clearly marked 'Paid in full.' Good-bye and keep well!" The men shook hands, and the Kraters departed.

"Our people validate the patients' insurance coverage and tabulate charges daily, so that checking out goes smoothly and quickly," Mr. Bradford observed.

"How long have you worked at Tri-City?" Steve asked.

"I started as an accounting assistant ten years ago. My two-year degree in accounting and experience as a legal stenographer qualified me for the position. Tri-City promotes from the ranks, so I worked hard toward that end. All the personnel in my department have the same opportunity. A high-school diploma, clerical skills and ambition are all that's required!" Mr. Bradford summed up.

Sam Rovner leaned back in the swivel chair and sucked on his favorite pipe. He and David Welpin were discussing staff participation in Tri-City's Fund Drive. "There's public interest in some of our new programs. Why not show the people how we spend their dollars?"

"We could start with our new approach to treating moderately disturbed patients, 'The Day Hospital,'" Mr. Welpin proposed.

Tri-City was known for its pioneering work in the

field of psychiatry, so it was not surprising that the hospital had one of the first day hospital programs in the state. Dr. Baer explained the program to Sam Rovner.

"We treat our patients during the day and send them home at night. Their day begins like most people's—except that, instead of leaving for a job five days a week, they come here! The day is carefully planned with therapy and activities with the hospital family. Come and see for yourself!" Dr. Baer invited. There were several activities in progress in a large, brightly decorated room.

Chad Merritt, a *Psychiatric Technician,* was sitting with two young men who were loudly debating the merits of baseball over football. Chad was a self-appointed referee to the amiable exchange. In keeping with the non-hospital-like environment, Chad wore street clothes instead of a uniform. This technician is part of the treatment plan; he observes, records and intervenes when necessary to provide for the therapeutic needs of patients. Chad worked with a group of six men and women. He planned and assisted with such group activities as patient government, occupational and recreational programs. He received $6,000 a year as a beginning technician.

Chad was qualified to participate as a coleader in planning and carrying out counseling and/or therapy groups. He was a graduate of a two-year program designed to train middle-level mental health workers. The A.A. (Associate of Arts) degree program offered courses

Auxiliary Services

in biological science, nursing, psychology, anatomy and physiology and group dynamics. A supervised field experience was part of the program. The broad curriculum was specific enough for a career student and yet provided flexibility for the transfer student to continue his studies in psychology or a related field. As Chad listened to the young men's argument, he was mentally making notes of their language, degree of animation and references to related and unrelated persons or activities. He would report these at the triweekly staff conference. Chad knew when to comment, when to remain silent or when to direct the men into another activity. During the patients' stay, he joined them at meals, play, therapy or prevocational counseling. Chad's observations of their actions and reactions would be of value to the psychiatrist-led team who carried out the treatment plan. Chad frequently worked with the *Psychiatric Aides,* who performed nursing procedures, assisted with medications and treatments and were supervised by the nursing staff. Their on-the-job training period lasted four months. Those desiring to continue their studies to become practical nurses found this experience helpful.

"That band really swings! Are you sure they're all amateurs?" Dave Welpin asked Roland Smith, *Therapeutic Recreation Assistant.*

"They're patients, and they're involved in the music and the activity. That's what we're trying to do! A few

CAREERS IN THE HEALTH FIELD

may have had professional training, but that's not important. My job is to help them develop satisfying recreational interests and skills."

About 30 men and women were dancing to the music; each was expressing himself through the music with various dance steps and body movements. "Want to dance?" asked a tall, thin girl wearing her long blonde hair in a single, thick braid.

"Go ahead," urged Mr. Smith. Dave Welpin dropped his clip board on a chair and followed the pretty girl.

Mr. Smith shook his head and smiled as he watched the two young people gyrate to the music. "She's improved; a year ago, she was our star wallflower!" he murmured to himself.

Mr. Smith was another member of the treatment team. He provided a wide variety of enjoyable activities for individual or groups of patients, often recommending specific physical or social recreative activities. He also planned and supervised supportive and special interest recreational programs for all the patients. Mr. Smith's programs included athletics, arts and crafts, hobbies, games, movies, dancing, parties, gardening and dramatic performances. At college, he had taken survey courses in anatomy, physiology and psychology. His other course work covered such areas as team sports, dance workshop, ceramics, costume design and sculpture. With an A.A.S. (Associate in Applied Science) degree, Mr. Smith's initial salary was $6,000 a year. However,

Auxiliary Services

he hoped to become a teacher in his field and attended evening classes to earn a bachelor's degree.

"How can your families help you stay 'clean'? You're about to join the day hospital program, which means that for 16 hours you'll be on your own!" Tracy Dowd, *Social Work Technician,* sat amid the group of drug abusers. The young adults, male and female, draped themselves over the furniture or sat on floor cushions. Miss Dowd, a treatment group member, was helping them prepare for the next step in their rehabilitation plan. Getting the patients to express their fears, doubts and hopes provided helpful information for the family contacts and home visits she made. Miss Dowd's supervisor was a social worker. To assist him, Miss Dowd performed many of the routine social work functions, such as intake interviewing, agency contacts and home visits.

Miss Dowd held a two-year college degree, which meant that she had successfully completed a health-core curriculum. While in college, she had learned about health and social agencies, principles of mental health, interviewing techniques and urban problems. She also took formal course work in abnormal psychology, biology, sociology and anthropology. She followed up her clients after their discharge, and, in cooperation with the *Community Mental Health Aide,* she continued to help them reach complete rehabilitation. The community worker attempts to bridge the gap in services between health professionals and between consumers' needs and service delivery programs.

"So far, the list has love, understanding, patience, employment, moral support, acceptance, warmth and respect. Now let's start on the difficult one—what can you do?" Miss Dowd challenged the group.

Mr. Welpin returned to his office and wrote a memo on his calendar. The memo referred to the three technicians needed in the psychiatric department; these professionals must be included in his next recruitment visit to the community college. He also noted that positions for these three would also be available in corrective and geriatric facilities. His secretary called on the interoffice telephone. "You have an appointment with Linda Cochrane in 20 minutes." Miss Cochrane was *Coordinator of Employees' Health Services*. Her office arranged for all new employees to have physical examinations, chest x-rays and laboratory tests. When an employee was ill or injured, she coordinated the employee's health activities with outside agencies, such as the Union Benefit Plan and Workmen's Compensation Board. Mr. Welpin reached Miss Cochrane's office with a minute to spare.

"Good afternoon, Mr. Welpin," said Penny Walker, the department's senior *Secretary/Typist*. Penny was typing the statistical report for the board of directors' meeting. The report contained frequency tables on incidents of employee illness, accident and death, common health

Auxiliary Services

problems of new employees and absentee rates for employees in stress areas, such as the operating rooms and emergency services.

Penny participated in Aldrich High's first cooperative plan and became a Tri-City employee immediately after graduation. She also acted as *Receptionist* and prepared the many forms for new employees to complete. Since Penny dealt with all areas of Tri-City, her knowledge of the hospital was extensive and her smiling responses reassured many timid new employees.

"It's been a while, Dave. Have a seat!" Miss Cochrane said in a slightly nasal New England accent. "I want your opinion about setting up sort of a day-care center for employees' children. I say 'sort of,' because I'd like to have only those youngsters who have health problems that cause my employee absentee rates to soar. These poor kids have things like sickle-cell anemia, rheumatic fever, allergies and asthma."

"If it's going to cost money, you're talking to the wrong man," Mr. Welpin said sympathetically.

"Not too much money, Dave. Hear me out, please," Miss Cochrane pleaded. "There's a new physician assistant–type program at the community college. We would provide clinical or field experience for the *Pediatric Assistant* and *Child Care Technician*—two of their associate degree programs. The children would receive much needed continuity in medical care, supervised play and social activities in a safe, healthy environment." Miss

CAREERS IN THE HEALTH FIELD

Cochrane held her breath. Mr. Welpin was scratching notes on her telephone pad!

"This *Pediatric Assistant* works under the supervision of a pediatrician?"

"Yes. He takes case histories, does routine physicals and follow-up examinations as needed, makes probable diagnoses, performs simple treatments and often makes home visits. Many of the men enrolled in the program are veterans with combat medic experience, but some other students are 'retired mothers' with previous college experience." Miss Cochrane took a catalogue from a bookcase and passed it to the personnel director. Mr. Welpin turned to the dog-eared pages and read silently, while Miss Cochrane quickly leafed through professional journals on her desk.

Mr. Welpin's voice broke the eerie quiet. "I see 'works under close supervision' is repeated several times. Since our setting is a hospital, this won't be a major consideration. The college courses include biological sciences, nutrition, growth and development, maternal and child care, dental hygiene and psychology. Field work includes the care of well children too."

Miss Cochrane pointed to the journals. "Here are reports of several such operations in other parts of the country. They write about two other paraprofessionals, the pediatric aide and the child care technician.

"So that the pediatric assistant can utilize his valuable time effectively, he needs the services of the *Pediatric*

Auxiliary Services

Aide. The aides greet and escort mothers and children from waiting areas to the examining and treatment rooms. Other tasks performed by aides include taking height and weight, temperatures, assisting with treatments and inoculations, child feeding, vision screening and some record keeping. Aides are usually supervised by pediatric assistants who plan the aides' four week on-the-job training program."

"That's an entry-level position at $2.25 an hour," Mr. Welpin remarked. "What about the *Child Care Technician?*"

Miss Cochrane turned the page of the catalogue. "This professional is trained to serve as assistant teacher in child day centers, preschool and other early childhood agencies," she read aloud.

Dave Welpin leaned forward. "You've got my vote of confidence, Linda—now let's prepare for our battle with the board!"

Twelve ▶

OUT IN THE COMMUNITY

The day was hot—almost 90 degrees and not quite noon! Mrs. Rodriguez clasped the squirming, damp baby closer to her chest and stepped down from the humid, crowded bus. She turned and reached for Felipe and Carmelita. The driver carefully handed each tot into Mrs. Rodriguez' outstretched arms. Her bloated abdomen, heavy with unborn child, made her steps mincing and awkward. The three blocks to the satellite clinic, Oak Street Health Center, seemed like a mile.

"*Buenos dias, señora! Como esta usted?*" a soft, lyrical voice inquired. Mrs. Rodriguez quietly replied in her native language. Rosalie García helped Mrs. Rodriguez to a chair and laid the gurgling baby in a bassinet with a disposable plastic liner. She dropped to one knee and in Spanish spoke to the little ones. "*Si, si!*" they chorused happily. Mrs García embraced them and led them off to the play area; the children were left in the care of an attendant.

Out in the Community

Mrs. García worked as a *Family Health Worker*. Her duties were performed in the clinic and in patients' homes. Because she was bilingual, familiar with patients' cultural and ethnic mores and a local resident, Mrs. García's services were vital to the smooth functioning of the clinic. She increased and encouraged communication between staff and patients which resulted in greater understanding and cooperation. Mrs. García accepted the expectant mother's urine specimen and assisted her onto the scale. "You gained only one pound this month: the doctor will be very pleased!" she said in Spanish. Mrs. García shook the thermometer sharply and placed it under Mrs. Rodriguez' tongue. Holding the patient's left wrist lightly, she felt for the pulse. "What food substitutions are you making in your diet?" she asked with one eye on the sweep hand of her watch. The family health worker continued to inquire about the patient's sleeping habits, activities, household duties and general comfort.

"Mrs. Rodriguez is ready, Dr. Konheim." Mrs. García escorted the paper-gowned patient into the examining room.

"Thank you," the doctor said and took the up-to-date chart from the aide.

Under the direction of a public health nurse, the family health worker receives four weeks of on-the-job training learning how to interview, take blood pressure and perform simple analytic urine tests. Maturity, interest in helping people, warmth and patience are personal characteristics required for this worker. Except for average reading and writing skills, there are no formal educational requirements. Family health workers are usually recruited from the neighborhoods around the clinic.

"I've brought Felipe and Carmelita for cleaning. Can you take them while their mother is in prenatal?" Mrs. García stood in the doorway of the dental clinic, the Rodriguez children clutching the skirt of her gray- and white-striped uniform.

Robin Buchanan, *Dental Hygienist,* consulted her appointment book. "Yes. I can. We had two 'no shows' this morning." Miss Buchanan led the children into the sunny yellow- and white-painted room; they raced toward the bright fireman's-red dental chairs. "Sit down and fasten your seatbelt, Carmelita! Felipe and I will give you a ride." Miss Buchanan and Felipe pumped hard on the floor pedal. Carmelita's happy shrieks grew louder as the chair rose higher.

Miss Buchanan was a licensed, professional oral-health educator. Working under the supervision of a dentist, she cleaned and polished children's teeth. As a dental hygienist, she taught patients about individual dental needs, methods of toothbrushing and gum care and prevention of oral disease. Miss Buchanan's friendly smile, cheerful disposition and love of children seduced even the most reluctant patient. She could calm a fretful child, reassure a frightened one and get another's cooperation during a painful treatment. Upon obtaining an A.A.S. (Applied

Associate in Science) degree, Miss Buchanan successfully passed a state examination which permitted her to practice dental hygiene. Dental hygienists also work in school systems and dentists' offices for salaries that begin as high as $8,700 a year.

Another member of the dental team is the *Dental Laboratory Technician*—the skilled craftsman of the dental world. These male and female technicians construct replacements for natural teeth which have been lost by disease or accident. The prosthetic (artificial) replacements include complete and partial dentures, crowns, porcelain restorations and orthodontic appliances. The diversified skills of this technican range from processing plastics to making castings of gold. Formal training for this career used to be on-the-job, but now most students enter two-year college programs. The A.A.S degree program includes courses in anatomy and physiology, ceramics, dental laboratory techniques and dental metallurgy in addition to those in liberal arts. Manual dexterity, good vision, artistic aptitudes and ability to follow specifications exactly as prescribed by the dentist are essential for one considering this career. Graduates of approved schools of dental technology may (after three years of additional experience) take the certification examination for dental technicians and become eligible to use the initials C.D.T. after their names. These technicians find employment with dentists or in commercial dental laboratories. By working with several dentists, a technician could earn as much as $9,000 to $12,000 a year.

"Mrs. Jackson—will you bring Sheila in now, please?" Midge Duncan, *Orthoptist,* called from her small cubicle. Sheila was to receive new eye muscle exercises. Miss Duncan held an A.A. (associate in arts) degree from a two-year college. To prepare for her profession, she spent an additional year of training in orthoptics (techniques for strengthening weakened eye muscles). Several years ago, Midge spent a summer as a counselor at a camp for handicapped children. She enjoyed working with the campers, and they loved her arts and crafts classes. For a while, Midge considered a career in elementary school teaching. But her cooperative experience at Tri-City Eye clinic changed those plans. The ophthalmologist (eye doctor) encouraged Midge to seek professional training. She was patient, well groomed, healthy, flexible and easygoing and had a sense of humor. Children were attracted to her and gave full cooperation to her instructions, which helped misaligned (off-center) eyes work together as they should.

When the treatment was completed, Miss Duncan took Sheila's hand and walked her over to Frank's shop. Frank Bernstein was the health center's *Optical Technician.* His responsibility was to set up and operate machines to grind eyeglass lenses to prescription specifications and assemble lenses in frames. Sheila was to be fitted for her new glasses

Out in the Community

today. "We'll take them to the optician for fitting if they're ready, Frank," Miss Duncan said. Frank had received Sheila's prescription from the ophthalmologist two weeks earlier. To fill the prescription, Frank read the lens and frame specifications, selected lenses from stock and mounted Sheila's lenses in frames. He often used such machines as generator, polisher, edger and hardener in his work.

Frank worked closely with the *Optician* in carrying out his duties. After Frank ground lenses, he consulted with the optician, who designed and fitted frames becoming to the wearer's features. Frank's training period extended over ten months, as compared with the two-year educational program completed by most opticians. Many community colleges offer an associate degree program in this specialty, which includes courses in geometric and mechanical optics, physiology of the eye, theory of contact lenses and visual aids in addition to liberal arts courses. Graduates are qualified to take a licensing examination for ophthalmic dispensing offered by most states. Licensure qualifies one for positions as contact lens technicians or ophthalmic dispensers or in optical laboratories. Optical technicians frequently advance to opticians because of the greater variety of employment opportunities. Both professions require good vision, mathematical aptitude and skill in the use of tools and instruments. The optical industry is growing rapidly, partly because of Medicare and other health programs.

Mrs. Rodriguez reread the appointment slip, which was written in Spanish. She was to report to the family-planning clinic next Wednesday. Mrs. García, the family health worker, explained that the purpose of this clinic was to educate and advise those interested in acceptable family-planning methods. The staff included a Family Planning Coordinator, two licensed practical nurses and four family planning counselors. Shelley Andrews, R.N., the *Coordinator,* held a bachelor's degree in community health education. She organized and administered the services of the free clinic. For health, social or financial reasons, the clients wanted healthy children spaced so as to enrich family stability. The women were referred by physicians, clinics, social agencies, hospitals and welfare case workers.

A *Family Planning Counselor* receives 60 hours of classroom training in addition to weekly in-service classes. Neither previous experience in a health care setting nor a high-school diploma are required; but a desire to help and work with people on a face-to-face basis, patience, understanding of subcultural mores and good health are important.

"Today, we're going to discuss the importance of follow-up in relation to clinic visits," Mrs. Andrews said as the class settled down.

Out in the Community

Mrs. Burroughs, one of the clinic's family-planning counselors, moved to the front of the room, opened a lined notebook and began. "The patient missed two clinic visits, so I went to the house. I found that she was taking some pills that a neighbor recommended, so she didn't think she needed any clinic. I explained the danger of taking medication not ordered for you by your own doctor. Because the pills worked for the neighbor, my patient's husband thought they were good and urged his wife to use them. We talked about fear of trying anything new, superstitions and how important it is for the husband to be part of successful family planning." Mrs. Burroughs stopped reporting and looked toward the coordinator.

"This visit shows the danger of partial information, the need for continuity in our services and the importance of total family participation," Mrs. Andrews observed.

Another offering of the health center is the services of the home health aide or homemaker. The function of the *Home Health Aide* is to provide assistance to family members during periods of illness, disability or absence. The disabled could be any family member. For example, the care of a multiple-handicapped child might, for a while, require the full attention of his mother; the aide would assist with the care of the other children and the housekeeping. If a parent is hospitalized, the aide often moves into the home to keep the family intact. A public health nurse provides the aides' four weeks of training in first aid, simple nursing procedures, diet planning and child care. Aides should be able to work with persons of all age groups and have unlimited patience, flexibility, stability and good health. Experienced aides, women or men, often advance to practical nurses with additional education and training.

Mrs. Rodriguez was one of many who benefited from this clinic service. When she reported for her scheduled appointment, the public health nurse called her in for a moment. "I have wonderful news for you!" she said. "A Spanish-speaking home health aide will care for the children and the house while you're hospitalized at Tri-City. She'll even stay an extra week when you come home with the baby!"

The health officer, Dr. Donald Hoskins, led the group toward the well-child clinic. The 15 men and women were *Teacher Aides* in training. All were high-school graduates who enjoyed working with children in an educational setting but were unable to devote more than two years to higher education at this time. Most were recruited from the local school area; some were parents of school-age children. For the next two years, the teacher aides, many of them Spanish-speaking, would divide their time between the community college and a neighborhood, elementary classroom. At the college, they studied such courses as biology, mental health, patterns of growth and

Out in the Community

development, child psychology and community services and resources. This education associate curriculum led to the A.A. degree, and many interested students hoped to continue their education towards a bachelor degree at a future date.

A teacher aide works in the classroom assisting the teacher and students. He not only relieves the teacher from routine clerical activities but actively participates in carrying out the educational program by working with small groups of children correcting homework and classwork and directing review and drill work.

"Today, you will see what constitutes a complete physical examination. You will also learn how even minor disability can influence a child's learning performance," Dr. Hoskins informed the group. The teacher aides separated into groups of three and observed the pediatricians at work in partitioned, curtained examining rooms. Earning while learning, these aides' beginning annual salaries were $7,500.

After he had completed his morning with the teacher aides, Dr. Hoskins sat quietly in his office studying his notes. At tonight's County Health Association meeting, he would deliver his committee's final report concerning careers in environmental health. Dr. Hoskins worked for several weeks with marine biologists, sanitation engineers, agronomists (crop production scientists) and public health personnel collecting data and developing job classifications. He read silently. "Environmental health

CAREERS IN THE HEALTH FIELD

technicians work with those responsible for maintaining the general health and welfare of the public. Graduates of two-year programs can find employment in several entry-level positions." The doctor passed the notes to his secretary. "Will you please edit these, Toba?" She took them and read.

"A *Health Laboratory Technician* does chemical and bacteriological analyses with samples of water, food and air. He works in a public health agency or sewage disposal plant. To protect diners in public eating places, the *Food Service Inspector* enforces local health laws; he makes spot checks on restaurants, luncheonettes and cafeterias. The *Sanitary Inspector* also visits public gathering places to see that public sanitation laws and regulations are followed. Firms that process and package drugs, meat, fish, dairy and other food products must follow legal standards. The *Food Products Inspector* visits these establishments to see that standards of sanitation, grading and purity are upheld. Sanitary engineers working in water supply, treatment and pollution need the assistance of *Health Engineering Assistants*."

Toba Henry, Dr. Hoskins' secretary, shuffled the typewritten notes. "What about licenses or certification? Are they needed?"

"Graduates of two-year programs are eligible to take civil service examinations leading to certification as environmental health technicians. Health departments require certification, but the trend is toward state certifica-

Out in the Community

tion or licensure," Dr. Hoskins replied. "A technician can advance to a sanitary engineer if he earns a bachelor's degree. Starting salaries are about $7,500 to $9,000 a year—probably higher in some industries."

Miss Henry rolled fresh paper into her typewriter. "I'll add the high-school course requirements of algebra, geometry, chemistry and physics. Because a technician has to make extensive reports, above-average ability in communication and writing skills are important. Potential technicians should possess the ability to relate to people, be able to follow rules, have good working habits and possess a sense of civic responsibility." She released the paper and clipped it to the rest of the doctor's notes.

No story of community health would be complete without mentioning the fast growing industry of nursing homes. According to the 1970 Census, 10 per cent of all people in the United States are 65 years old or older—and the number of older people is on the rise, with sharp increases in the over–75-year-old group! Elderly people not only are more likely to have long-term illnesses but also face the difficulty of paying medical and hospital bills out of reduced incomes. Medicare and Medicaid and federal and federal-state programs, permit the aged to receive comprehensive health care services free or at reduced costs. These plans and other extensive legislation have been enacted to meet the growing need for nursing home facilities and services for the aging. Unlike a hospital, where the staff and services focus on treating a particular illness or injury, a nursing home must consider the whole patient in its treatment plan, and usually for a much longer period of time.

"When do you expect the new nursing home to open?" Bob Youman asked Dave Welpin. Mr. Youman was an *Employment Counselor* at the County Employment Services.

"We plan to admit the first 50 patients within two months if we can find suitable staff. Although people live for longer periods now, medical science still hasn't solved many of the problems of old age, like arthritis, hardening of the arteries and senility. We'll need a staff that can provide custodial and rehabilitative care."

"Let's decide on classifications first," Mr. Youman suggested.

"Administrative, nursing and supportive services, rehabilitative, social services and maintenance personnel are the categories found in most nursing homes."

The *Administrator* is responsible for over-all management and must coordinate the work of all personnel to assure efficient and productive operation of the facility. Management skills and understanding of sound business practices, learned through experience and formal course work, are required for this highly demanding position. Most administrators are graduates of business colleges, and some possess graduate degrees in nursing-home administration, a new curriculum available at some uni-

Out in the Community

versities. His *Assistant* assumes responsibility for several departments, and needs similar qualifications, but to a lesser degree. A *Business Manager* is usually included in the administrative staff. His responsibility is to supervise and direct accounting, admitting and credit and collection functions. He maintains financial records, assists in budget preparation, compiles financial reports, prepares payrolls and performs other related bookkeeping functions. A two- or four-year degree in business administration or accounting prepares one for this position.

Mr. Welpin broke in on the employment counselor's thoughts. "You'll need a *Director of Nursing* services with administrative and supervisory experience. He or she must be imaginative enough to develop specific nursing programs for each patient according to his needs. The population of a nursing home often ranges from the completely ambulatory patient to the bed-ridden invalid, and the director works closely with a staff of registered and practical nurses, dietitians, aides and attendants. We are planning flexible units on each floor, to provide for a variety of age groups and degrees of disability.

Mr. Youman rose and ambled toward the filing cabinets. "I think I may have someone for that position. Her references repeatedly noted incidences of understanding, gentleness, compassion and ability to handle difficult situations. She's had extensive geriatrics [medical specialty dealing with the hygiene and diseases of old age] experience too!"

CAREERS IN THE HEALTH FIELD

Mr. Welpin shifted to the edge of the chair. "That's what I mean, Bob! The whole staff should have those qualities! Our patients are generally lonely, sick elderly people with real and imaginary fears. Our mission is to bring some sunshine into their lives!"

"I feel the therapists should be special people too! You'll need physical, occupational and recreational therapists. Is it true that they'll have a gym and a sauna?"

"Everyone will have an activity program of some kind. There will be cook-outs and picnics on the grounds. Boat rides in summer! Bus trips to the state parks! Our mini-kitchens on each floor will permit a grandmother to continue baking cookies for her grandchildren. The Hobby Shop volunteers will teach and encourage a wide range of crafts."

During the next hour, the two men discussed the other staff needs and ways of meeting them. Many of the policies of Tri-City would be applicable to the nursing home, such as the policy of upgrading and promotion from within departments. Salaries would match those paid to hospital employees in similar positions, and the cooperative plan with Aldrich High would operate in the nursing home, too.

It was almost dusk when Bob Youman turned the key in the lock of his office door. The long carpeted hallway muffled the two men's steps as they advanced to the elevators. Each was deeply immersed in his own thoughts. Dave Welpin broke the silence. "Bob, I'm sure our nursing home will be a happy place! Say, you'll be a senior citizen in about 2011! How about making a reservation right now?" Both chuckled softly and stepped into the waiting elevator.

LOOKING AHEAD

You've read the book and now you're wondering. "Perhaps there is a career for me in health science. It sounds good now, but what will the field be like 10 years from now or even five?" Suppose we take a look at some recent findings. We'll begin with some of the projections of the preliminary report by the Carnegie Commission on Higher Education, *Higher Education and the Nation's Health*. The report, widely circulated, was acclaimed as highly distinguished by educators and government agencies.

> We read that the rate of acquisition of new knowledge and technology in the biomedical sciences will continue at an accelerated pace.
> Progress in diagnosis and therapy, involving increasingly complex facilities, as well as trained technicians will continue at a rapid rate.
> The most important impact on the health care system will come from extensive use of computers and automation techniques in institutional administration and patient care facilities.

Looking Ahead

New therapeutic techniques will require new technologies, new kinds of trained personnel and greater emphasis on achieving effective functioning of health care teams.

The government's role in protecting the health of the population will become broader in scope. Its activities will include a more comprehensive national health system and the utilization of health manpower.

As a result of the tremendous progress that has been made in overcoming and, in many cases, eliminating sources of acute illness, concern has shifted to the prevention of disease, diagnosis and treatment of degenerative diseases and mental illness. Each of these will be affected by major developments in the next few decades.

There will be a shift to greater emphasis on care outside the hospital in a wider variety of health care facilities. These will include neighborhood health clinics, facilities for ambulatory care of convalescing patients and homemaker services.

In other words, as advancements in medical science continue, the need and demand for highly skilled health manpower will keep pace. In some cases, traditional training for nurses, dietitians and laboratory science personnel will be replaced with reforms in affiliation, period of study and type of curriculum.

CAREERS IN THE HEALTH FIELD

In this book, you learned of some health occupations that were unknown 20 years ago but are now well established, such as the Inhalation Therapist, the Prosthesist and the Cytotechnologist. This trend will continue. Some will be entirely new occupations such as the Extracorporeal Circulation Specialist. Others will be offshoots of an existing occupation; the Physician's Assistant is one example.

Significant changes in America's manpower posture will be reflected in new occupational titles, new training programs in schools and hospitals and new educational requirements. Post high school training, such as that obtained through on-the-job training and junior and community colleges, will take on increasing importance. The number of professional and technical positions, those that usually require a college degree, will continue to grow. However 4 out of every 5 jobs to be filled in the next decade will be filled with persons who have less than four years of college education.

Most of these new occupations are at the aide, assistant and technician level—the allied health level, which represents some 85 percent of all health workers. Emerging occupations include the Anesthesiological Assistant, the Optometric Technician, the Animal Health Technologist, the Urological Assistant, the Radiopharmacist, the Dialysis Assistant, the Genetic Assistant and the Social Rehabilitation Service Worker. The Bureau of Labor Statistics of the Department of Labor predicts that service industries, which include the health field, will con-

Looking Ahead

tinue to be among the fastest growing industries through the mid-1980's. Manpower requirements in health services are expected to grow rapidly due to the increasing ability of persons to pay for health care.

New developments in the use of automation and electronics in the health field offer a view of the future. One example is the extensive use of computers which will bring better health care and new categories of jobs such as operation, maintenance, and repair of equipment. Others include Monitoring Consoles and Automatic Chemical Analyzers. Electronic devices are being installed in hospitals to scan X-rays, enlarge them, read them and convert them for storage and easy retrieval. It is now possible to send images over wires for reading, thus enabling remote areas to benefit from expert medical advice.

The health service's growth is expected to accelerate rather than slow down. Some 4 million people are involved in the field today. By 1980, there are expected to be at least 6 million engaged in some area of health. Women will be found in traditionally male-oriented careers such as those in medical specialties, environmental engineering and medical computer sciences.

Health services can take you anywhere. You can stay in your hometown. If you do not want to remain in your city or state, there is practically no limit on choices in any other part of this country, or another country, or even in outer space.

SOURCES OF FURTHER INFORMATION

If you would like to learn more about the careers discussed in this book, please write directly to the organizations listed.

CHAPTER TWO

Certified Laboratory Assistant
American Association of Blood Banks
30 No. Michigan Avenue—Suite 1322
Chicago, Illinois 60602

Medical Laboratory Technology—Cytotechnology
American Society For Medical Technology
555 West Loop South
Houston, Texas 77401

American Medical Technologists
710 Higgins Road
Park Ridge, Illinois 60068

Registry of Medical Technologists (ASCP)
P.O. Box 4872
Chicago, Illinois 60680

Nat'l Committee for Careers in Medical Laboratory
9650 Rockville Pike
Bethesda, Maryland 20014

Histologic Technology
Council on Medical Education of the American Medical
    Association
535 North Dearborn Street
Chicago, Illinois 60610

Certified Laboratory Assistant
Board of Certified Laboratory Assistants
445 North Lake Shore Drive
Chicago, Illinois 60611

Electroencephalographic Technician
American Board of Registration of Electroencephalographic
    Technologists
Cleveland Clinic
9500 Euclid Avenue
Cleveland, Ohio 44105

Sources of Further Information

Electrocardiograph and Electromyograph Technicians
American Hospital Association
840 North Lake Shore Drive
Chicago, Illinois 60681

Pathologist Assistant
American Assoc. of Pathologists and Bacteriologists
260 Crittendon Boulevard
Rochester, New York 14620

American Society of Clinical Pathologists
2100 West Harrison Street
Chicago, Illinois 60612

OTHER GENERAL REFERENCES

American Institute of Biological Sciences
3900 Wisconsin Avenue, N.W.
Washington, D.C. 20016

American Society of Microbiology
1913 Eye Street, N.W.
Washington, D.C. 20006

International Society of Clinical Laboratory Technicians
805 Ambassador Building
411 No. Seventh Street
St. Louis, Missouri 63101

CHAPTER THREE

Nurse, Licensed Practical
National Association for Practical Nurse Education and
    Service, Inc.
122 East 42 Street   Suite 800
New York, New York 10017

National Federation of Licensed Practical Nurses, Inc.
250 West 57 Street
New York, New York 10019

Nurse, Registered Professional
National League for Nursing, Inc.
Committee on Nursing Careers
10 Columbus Circle
New York, New York 10019

Operating Room Technician
Surgical Technician
The Association of Operating Room Technicians, Inc.
1100 West Littleton Boulevard   Suite 101
Littleton, Colorado 80120

CAREERS IN THE HEALTH FIELD

Nurses' Aide/Orderlie/Attendant
American Hospital Association
840 North Lake Shore Drive
Chicago, Illinois 60611

Biomedical Equipment Technician
National Kidney Foundation
116 East 27 Street
New York, New York 10016

OTHER GENERAL REFERENCES
American Physiological Society
9650 Rockville Pike
Bethesda, Maryland 20014

CHAPTER FOUR

Biomedical Engineering and Instrumentation
Division of Research Services—NIH
9000 Wisconsin Avenue
Bethesda, Maryland 20014

Biomedical Engineering Society
P.O. Box 1600
Evanston, Illinois 60204

Occupational Therapy Assistant
American Occupational Therapy Association ✓
6000 Executive Boulevard
Rockville, Maryland 20852

Orthopedic Assistant
American Academy of Orthopedic Surgeons
450 North Michigan Avenue
Chicago, Illinois 60611

Physical Therapy Technician/Assistant
The American Physical Therapy Association
1156 15th Street N.W.
Washington, D.C. 20005

Radiation Therapy Technologist
Nuclear Medicine Technologist
American Society of Radiological Technologists
645 North Michigan Avenue
Chicago, Illinois 60611

OTHER GENERAL REFERENCES
American Academy of Physical Medicine and Rehabilitation
30 North Michigan Avenue
Chicago, Illinois 60602

Sources of Further Information

American Orthoptic & Prosthetic Association
1440 N Street N.W.
Washington, D.C. 20005

Association for Physical & Mental Rehabilitation
105 Saint Lawrence Street
Rehoboth Beach, Delaware 19971

National Easter Seal Society for Crippled Children & Adults
2023 West Ogden Avenue
Chicago, Illinois 60612

CHAPTER FIVE

Biomedical Engineering and Instrumentation
Division of Research Services NIH
9000 Wisconsin Avenue
Bethesda, Maryland 20014

Biomedical Engineering Society
P.O. Box 1600
Evanston, Illinois 60204

Inhalation Therapist
American Association for Inhalation Therapy
3554 Ninth Street
Riverside, California 92501

Pharmacy Assistant
American Society of Hospital Pharmacists
4630 Montgomery Avenue
Washington, D.C. 20014

American Pharmaceutical Association
2215 Constitution Avenue, N.W.
Washington, D.C. 20037

X-Ray Technology
American Society of Radiologic Technologists
645 North Michigan Avenue
Chicago, Illinois 60611

American Registry of Radiologic Technicians
2600 Wayzata Boulevard
Minneapolis, Minnesota 55405

OTHER GENERAL REFERENCES

American National Red Cross
17th and D Streets, N.W.
Washington, D.C. 20006

Division of Careers and Recruitment
American Hospital Association
840 North Lake Shore Drive
Chicago, Illinois 60611

CAREERS IN THE HEALTH FIELD

Society of Nuclear Medicine
211 East 43 Street
New York, New York 10017

Society of Nuclear Medical Technologists
1201 Waukegan Road
Glenview, Illinois 60025

CHAPTER SIX

Dietician, Dietary Aide/Technician
American Dietetic Association
620 North Michigan Avenue
Chicago, Illinois 60611

American Home Economics Association
2010 Massachusetts Avenue, N.W.
Washington, D.C. 20036

Institute of Food Technologists
221 North La Salle Street — Suite 2120
Chicago, Illinois 60601

International Association of Milk, Food & Environmental Sanitarians, Inc.
P.O. Box 437
Shelbyville, Indiana 46176

Executive Housekeeper
The National Executive Housekeepers Association, Inc.
Business and Professional Building
Second Avenue
Gallipolis, Ohio 45631

Laundry Careers
American Institute of Laundering
Institutional Division
Joliet, Illinois 60434

Unit Clerk
American Association of Medical Assistants, Inc.
One East Wacker Drive — Suite 1510
Chicago, Illinois 60001

CHAPTER SEVEN

Medical Clerk/Secretary/Transcriber
American Association of Medical Assistants, Inc.
One East Wacker Drive — Suite 1510
Chicago, Illinois 60001

American Medical Association Council on Medical Education
535 North Dearborn Street
Chicago, Illinois 60610

Sources of Further Information

American Medical Record Association
John Hancock Center — Suite 1850
875 North Michigan Avenue
Chicago, Illinois 60611

CHAPTER EIGHT

Admitting Officer
American Hospital Association
840 North Lake Shore Drive
Chicago, Illinois 60611

Hospital Administration
American College of Hospital Administrators
840 North Lake Shore Drive
Chicago, Illinois 60611

Association of University Programs in Hospital
 Administration
One Dupont Circle
Washington, D.C. 20036

Medical Assistant
American Association of Medical Assistants, Inc.
One East Wacker Drive — Suite 1510
Chicago, Illinois 60001

Public Health Nurse
American Nurses' Association
2420 Pershing Road
Kansas City, Missouri 64108

U.S. Office of Education
Division of Vocational and Technical Education
Health Occupations
Washington, D.C. 20202

Public Health Service
National Institutes of Health, Information Office
Office of Public Inquiries
Bethesda, Maryland 20034

Social Worker, Aide/Technician
National Commission for Social Work Careers
2 Park Avenue
New York, New York 10016

American Sociological Association
1722 N Street, N.W.
Washington, D.C. 20036

National Association of Social Workers
2 Park Avenue
New York, New York 10016

183

CAREERS IN THE HEALTH FIELD
OTHER GENERAL REFERENCES

Association of Schools of Allied Health Professions
One Dupont Circle — Suite 300
Washington, D.C. 20036

Hospital Financial Management Association
840 North Lake Shore Drive
Chicago, Illinois 60611

CHAPTER NINE

Central Supply Technician
American Society for Hospital Central Service Personnel
840 North Lake Shore Drive
Chicago, Illinois 60611

Hospital Engineering and Maintenance
American Society for Hospital Engineering
840 North Lake Shore Drive
Chicago, Illinois 60611

American Society of Safety Engineers
850 Busse Highway
Park Ridge, Illinois 60068

National Safety Council
425 North Michigan Avenue
Chicago, Illinois 60611

Engineers Joint Council
345 East 47 Street
New York, New York 10017

Institute of Sanitation Management
P.O. Box 462
Hicksville, New York 11802

American Industrial Hygiene Association
25711 Southfield Road
Southfield, Michigan 48075

National Environmental Health Association, Inc.
1600 Pennsylvania Avenue
Denver, Colorado 80203

CHAPTER TEN

Medical Record Librarian/Technician
American Medical Record Association
875 North Michigan Avenue
Chicago, Illinois 60611

Sources of Further Information

Medical Library Association, Inc.
919 North Michigan Avenue — Suite 2023
Chicago, Illinois 60611

Public Relations Officer
American Society for Hospital Public Relations Directors
840 North Lake Shore Drive
Chicago, Illinois 60611

Volunteer Services
American Hospital Association
840 North Lake Shore Drive
Chicago, Illinois 60611

OTHER GENERAL REFERENCES

Association of Medical Illustrators
Medical College of Georgia
Augusta, Georgia 30902

Biological Photographic Association
P.O. Box 12866
Philadelphia, Pennsylvania 19108

National Center for Health Services, Research &
   Development
5600 Fishers Lane
Rockville, Maryland 20852

Society of Technical Writers & Publishers
1010 Vermont Avenue, N.W.
Washington, D.C. 20005

CHAPTER ELEVEN

Hospital Business Careers
Hospital Financial Management Association
840 North Lake Shore Drive
Chicago, Illinois 60611

The American Statistical Association
810 18th Street, N.W.
Washington, D.C. 20006

Physicians' Assistant
American Association of Physicians' Assistants
Box 2914 CHS
Duke University Medical Center
Durham, North Carolina 27706

Psychiatric Technician/Aide
National Association of Psychiatric Technology
11th and L Building, Main Floor
Sacramento, California 95814

CAREERS IN THE HEALTH FIELD

National Association for Mental Health
1800 North Kent Street
Rosslyn, Virginia 22209

Therapeutic Recreation Assistant·
Therapeutic Recreation Services of the National Recreation ✓
& Park Association
1700 Pennsylvania Avenue, N.W.
Washington, D.C. 20006

OTHER GENERAL REFERENCES

American Association of Hospital Accountants
840 North Lake Shore Drive
Chicago, Illinois 60611

National Association for Music Therapy, Inc.
P. O. Box 610
Lawrence, Kansas 66044

American Journal of Art Therapy
Box 4918
Washington, D.C. 20008

CHAPTER TWELVE

Careers in Community Health
American Public Health Association
1015 18th Street N.W.
Washington, D.C. 20036

U.S. Office of Education
Division of Vocational and Technical Education
Health Occupations
Washington, D.C. 20202

Public Health Service
National Institutes of Health Information Office
Office of Public Inquiries
Bethesda, Maryland 20034

National Association for Mental Health
1800 Kent Stret
Rosslyn, Virginia 22209

American Association for Health, Physical Education & ✓
Recreation
National Education Association
1201 16th Street N.W.
Washington, D.C. 20036

American Public Health Association
1015 18th Street, N.W.
Washington, D.C. 20036

186

Sources of Further Information

Careers in Environmental Health
Personnel Office
Food and Drug Administration
U.S. Department of Health, Education and Welfare
Washington, D.C. 20204

Office of Manpower Development and Training
Environmental Health Service, PHS
Department of Health, Education, and Welfare
5600 Fishers Lane
Rockville, Maryland 20852

American Industrial Hygiene Association
25711 Southfield Road
Southfield, Michigan 48075

American Public Health Association
1015 18th Street, N.W.
Washington, D.C. 20030

National Sanitation Foundation
P.O. Box 1468
Ann Arbor, Michigan 48106

Dental Hygienist/Laboratory Technician
The Council on Dental Education
American Dental Association
211 East Chicago Avenue
Chicago, Illinois 60611

American Dental Hygienists Association
1101 17th Street, N.W.
Washington, D.C. 20036

National Association of Certified Dental Laboratories
3501 Mount Vernon Avenue
Alexandria, Virginia 20305

Nursing Home Careers

American Nursing Home Association
1025 Connecticut Avenue — Suite 607
Washington, D.C. 20036

National Council on the Aging
1828 L Street, N.W.
Washington, D.C. 20036

Optician/Technician
American Optometric Association
7000 Chippewa
St. Louis, Missouri 63119

CAREERS IN THE HEALTH FIELD

American Academy of Optometry
Foshay Tower
Minneapolis, Minnesota 55402

American Optometric Foundation
201 South Central Avenue
Clayton, Missouri 63105

Orthopist
The American Orthoptic Council
3400 Massachusetts Avenue N.W.
Washington, D.C. 20007

Personnel Director
American Society for Hospital Personnel Directors
840 North Lake Shore Drive
Chicago, Illinois 60611

Teacher Aide
Office of Education
U.S. Department of Health, Education and Welfare
400 Maryland Avenue S.W.
Washington, D.C. 20202

OTHER GENERAL REFERENCES
National Rehabilitation Counseling Association
1522 K Street, N.W.
Washington, D.C. 20005

American College of Nurse-Midwives
50 East 92 Street
New York, New York 10028

Planned Parenthood-World Population
810 Seventh Avenue
New York, New York 10019

Society for Public Health Education
655 Sutter Street
San Francisco, California 94102

American Corrective Therapy Association
5806 Gloucester Lane
Austin, Texas 78723

American Rehabilitation Counseling Association
1605 New Hampshire Avenue N.W.
Washington, D.C. 20009

INDEX

Account representative, 146
Admitting, assistant director of, 104
Admitting clerk, 105, 109
Admitting Offices, director of, 104
Air-conditioning installation and maintenance man, 120
American Association of Medical Record Librarians, 137
American Board of Registration of Electroencephalographic Technologists, 31
American College of Radiology, 67
American Medical Association, 34, 36
American Medical Technologists, 35
American Orthotic and Prosthetics Association, 54
American Registry of Inhalation Therapists, 69
American Registry of Radiological Technologists, 55, 67
American Society of Clinical Pathologists, 36
Anderson, Sarah, 124
Andrews, Shelley, 164
Anesthesiological assistant, 176
Area supervisor, 73
Asti, Gloria, 125
Attendant, 18, 24, 43

Bagley, Alfred, 117
Bard, Janice, 19
Beams, Ted, 48
Bernstein, Frank, 162
Biller, 145

Biomedical engineering technician, 65
Biomedical equipment technician, 46, 65
Boiler cook, 78
Boothe, Charles, 86
Bowman, Stephan, 16
Brennan, Tom, 20-21
Buchanan, Robin, 160
Business manager, 171
Byers, Mrs. Florence, 22

Cardiopulmonary technician, 63
Carpenter, 120
Carter, Gilbert, 29
Central supplies, director of, 124
Central supply assistant, 126
Central supply technician, 125
Certified laboratory assistant, 34
Chef, executive, 81
Chief hospital administrator, 130
Child care technician, 155, 157
City investigator, 147
Cleaner, general, 74
Clerk, general, 94
Cochrane, Linda, 154
Coleman, Sylvia, 141
Community mental health aide, 153
Computer programmer, 93
Control clerk, 148
Cook, apprentice, 81
Coronary care unit, 63
Cytotechnologist, 35-36

Dental hygienist, 160

189

Index

Dental laboratory technician, 161
Diet aide, 26, 78
Dietary technician, 27, 79
Dietician, administrative, 78, 80
Disraeli, Benjamin, 16
Donohue, Darren, 129
Doorman, 108
Dowd, Tracy, 153
Downey, Keith, 22
Duncan Midge, 162

Electrician's helper, 120
Electrocariograph technician, 30-31
Elevator operator, 111
Employees' health services, coordinator of, 154
Employment counselor, 170
Extractors, 77

Family health worker, 159
Family planning coordinator, 164
Family planning counselor, 164
Fergus, Beth, 131
Ferguson, Chandler, 144
Fields, Jim, 61
Flagg, Ron, 104
Floor buffer, 122
Floor waxer, 74
Food handler, general, 78
Food products inspector, 168
Food service inspector, 168
Forde, Dr. Harrison, 136
Fulton, Frank, 27-28
Furniture mover, 122
Furniture repairman and refinisher, 120

García, Rosalie, 158
Gould, Pam, 109

Haber, Robert, 137
Hairston, Stacey, 99, 100
Harley, Shirley, 139
Health engineering assistant, 168
Health field, careers in administrative workers, 86-98; hospital admissions staff, 99-114; hospital auxiliary services, 144-157; clerical staff for hospital, 86-98; communications area of health services, 129-143; community health services, 158-173; emergency care personnel, 59-71; extra-hospital health careers, 158-173; future of, 174-177; institutional housekeeping, 72-85; hospital maintenance staff, 72-85, 115-128; Open House Week at hospital, 39-47; case history involving typical services, 17-28; hospital public relations, 129-143; hospital security, 115-128; technical careers, generally, 29-37; careers in therapeutic work, 48-58
Health laboratory technician, 168
Higher Education and the Nation's Health, 174
Histologic technician, 34
Home health aide, 165
Housekeeper, executive, 72
Hyperbaric operator, 135

Inhalation therapist, 26, 68-69
Intravenous nurse, 110

Index

Jaffee, Barney, 63
Jarmón, Cheryl, 110

Kerns, Dr. Mel, 99
Kimmel, Gary, 132
Knox, Angela, 101-102

Laboratory technician, 21
Light man, 120
Linen room handler, 77
Locksmith, 124
Lyman, Phil, 115

Maid, 74
Maintenance and engineering, chief of, 117, 124
Major, Ivan, 133
Manager, assistant, 77
Marechal, Frederick, 130
McBain, Leslie, 135
Medical assistant, 101
Medical emergency technician, 17, 61
Medical laboratory technician, 35
Medical record librarian, chief, 137
Medical record technician, 137
Medical transcriber, 90
Messenger, 50, 109
Metal cleaner and polisher, 121
Miles, Sandy, 25
Moore, Lynette, 60

Nurse in charge, 22
Nurse, practical, 22, 39-40
Nurse, registered, 39-41
Nursing, director of, 171
Nursing supervisor, 60
Nurse's aide, 24, 26, 42

Occupational therapist assistant, 51-53
Occupational therapy aide, 27
Office machine serviceman, 121
O'Hara, Bill, 105
Operating room attendant, 21
Operating room technician, 22, 44-45
Optical technician, 162
Optician, 163
Orderly, 21, 42
Orthopedic assistant, 25, 27, 50
Orthoptist, 162
Orthotic technician, 27
Orthotist, 53

Packer, 77
Packer, Willis, 106
Page operator, 140
Painter, 118
Painter foreman, 118
Painter, touch-up, 122
Pastry cook, 78
Pathologist's assistant, 37
Patient accounts, director of, 145
Patient services, administrative assistant in charge of, 112
Pediatric aide, 156-157
Pediatric assistant, 155-156
Perkins, Dr. Michael, 18
Perkins, Donald, 33
Personnel director, 29
Pharmacy technician, 69-70
Photographer, 132
Physical therapy assistant, 27
Physical therapy technician, 48
Plasterer, 120
Plumber, 117
Plumber's helper, 118
Practical nurse, 22, 39-40

191

Index

Preadmitting clerk, 106
Prep team, 20
Price, Dr. Otto, 46
Printing assistant, 129
Projectionist, 133
Prosthetics assistant, 54
Public health nurse, 100
Public relations officer, 130
Public relations officer, assistant to, 132
Puller, 77
Purchasing agent, chief, 122
Psychiatric aide, 151
Psychiatric technician, 149

Quiet Zone, The, 37

Radiological technologist, 55
Randall, Jane, 51
Randall, Kirby, 55
Reade, Glen, 50-51
Receptionist, 141, 155
Refrigeration mechanic, 120
Rehabilitation therapist, 49
Registered nurse, 39-41
Reservation clerk, 104
Reservation clerk, chief, 106
Reuben, Jason, 56
Rohan, Mrs. Bella, 72
Rosado, Andy, 26
Rovner, Sam, 130

Salad man, 78, 81
Sanitary inspector, 168
Schuler, Dr. Martin, 61
Seamstress, 77
Seamstress, head, 77
Secretary, executive, 131
Secretary, medical, 92
Secretary/typist, 154
Security, chief of, 115
Security guard, 116

Sedgwick, Earl, 54
Senior resident, 18
Shade and drapery man, 121
Social service aide, 28
Social worker, 114
Social work technician, 27, 153
Sorters, 76
Soup cook, 78
Stenotypist, 90
Student nurse, 19
Surgical technician, 24
Switchboard operator, 139

Teacher aide, 166
Teasdale, Milton, 122
Television service and repairman, 121
Therapeutic recreation assistant, 151
Thompson, Ronald, 126
Tile setters, 120
Tile workers, 120
Transporter, 108
Tulane, Craig, 63
Typist/clerk, 94

Unit clerk, 72, 94, 97-98
Urological assistant, 176
Utilities mechanic, 120

Vegetable cook, 78
Volunteer association, 142

Walker, Penny, 154
Washer, 77
Wong, Sue, 21

X-ray technician, 23, 66

Young, Florence, 78
Youman, Bob, 170

APR 26 '77
FEB 20 '80
MAY 6 '80
OCT 12 '81
NOV 10 '81
SEP 8
APR 4
MAY 6 1987

DATE DUE